Let Me Encourage You Today

Daily Devotions

By Mark Beaird

To find out more about the ministry of Pastor Mark Beaird log on to: www.markbeaird.org or write to:

Mark Beaird Ministries
P.O. Box 43251
Birmingham, Alabama 35243

Cover photograph by Mark Beaird

Foreword

The author is a pastor, a media minister and writer of note. His devotionals have been published in several newspapers, including my own local newspaper. He has authored several books of sermons and maintains a web site.

This book of devotions will prove to be a blessing to both clergy and laypersons. It will provide many inspirational and instructional moments with God for all who study and meditate on its contents.

The Apostle Paul's declaration of love and exhortation recorded in 1 Timothy 1:5 is applicable to the author, Mark Beaird. A paraphrased rendering of this passage would read, "When I remember your sincere faith; which dwelt first in your grandmother Grace, and in your mother Doris; and I am persuaded dwells in you."

Mark has the heart, heritage, devotedness and giftedness to author such an insightful, inspirational and practical book of devotions.

> Hubert P. Black
> President Emeritus, Asian Seminary
> of Christian Ministries
> Gaylord Lambdin Chair of Education,
> Lincoln Memorial University

Preface

In each of these devotions, as with each newspaper column I write, the thoughts presented here are done so in a manner that will hopefully convey the relevance of the Christian faith to the believer and unbeliever alike. Jesus Christ is the one that can add meaning, life, hope and more to the human existence as well as giving eternal salvation for the soul. All one need to do is to place his or her trust in him. It is my prayer that, in reading these devotions, someone will see the truth and the relevance of the Christian faith as never before and choose to place his or her trust in Jesus Christ.

Dedication

To my wife and the love of my life, Elaine
Your faith led me to Christ
Your encouragement led me to try

Day 1

GOD HELPS THOSE WHO CANNOT HELP THEMSELVES

Wait a minute. That is not what we've heard all our lives. Is it not, "God helps those who help themselves?" That may be what we have always heard and said, but that's not what the Bible teaches. In fact, that age-old philosophy is dangerously close to the idea of salvation by works and grace by merit—not to mention the idea that some how God needs to be motivated to help us.

First of all, we know according to Ephesians 2:8-10 that it is by the grace of God that we are saved. Paul wrote, "For by grace you have been saved through faith, and that not of yourselves; it is the gift of God, not of works, lest anyone should boast. For we are His workmanship, created in Christ Jesus for good works, which God prepared beforehand that we should walk in them." (NKJ) Put aside the idea that somehow you and the "Good Lord" are responsible for your salvation. It's all Him! He did not just help you out. He did it all for you!

Now I realize that we must be willing to pray and exercise our faith by our actions—like Jesus said, "ask, seek and knock" (Matt. 7:7-12). That's participation in our salvation. But even the provision we find through those means is given to us by the grace of God, not because of something we have done to merit His participation in our lives. Somehow too many Christian people have adopted this idea that we have to give God a reason to help us, before and after salvation. He needs no reason other than that He loves us.

Someone put it just right when they said, "People need love, especially when they do not deserve it." We need to get past this pull-yourself-up-by-your-bootstraps-religion and realize that we are not self-made people. We cannot earn the blessings of God. As Psalms 100:3 says, "Know ye that the LORD he is God: it is he that hath made us, and not we ourselves; we are his people, and the sheep of his pasture." (KJV)

Too often we fail to think about such a message or philosophy may sound to those who are hopelessly lost without God. There are countless souls who would love to know God, but they think they must "do better" in order to be accepted. We who know Christ need to convey the truth of the matter no matter how it makes us look. The truth about us all is Romans 5:6 which says, "For when we were still without strength, in due time Christ died for the ungodly." (NKJ)

At one point in time, we were all without the strength to save ourselves. We were hopeless sinners. But "saint" or "sinner" there never will come a point in our lives that we do not need HIM supremely. God is not in the business of just helping those who can help themselves. He's in the business of helping those who cannot help themselves, but who want help desperately. He is in the business of helping those who do not know what to do. His grace is so amazing because it reaches out to all who will receive it, whether he or she is able to help themselves or not. Let me encourage you today to call upon the Lord. His strength is sufficient even if yours is not.

Day 2

WHY I DO WHAT I DO

For those who have labored faithfully for years in various church and ministry related positions, the idea of quitting because no one seems to care might be an idea that you have entertained before. I was reminded of this one day as I was talking to a successful minister friend of mine in another state. To my surprise the conversation centered on his desire to leave the ministry because he did not feel that he was accomplishing anything.

We see many examples in the Bible of people who felt this way, but Jeremiah stands out in my mind more than any of the others. Listen to his words in Jeremiah 20:9, "But if I say, 'I will not mention him or speak any more in his name,' his word is in my heart like a fire, a fire shut up in my bones. I am weary of holding it in; indeed, I cannot." (NIV)

Jeremiah was facing the ultimate tough crowd. First, the majority of them had no intention of listening much less changing. Secondly, not only did they not care about his message, but they also were prepared to take the necessary action to shut him up. The thought of just quitting must have eaten at him—and why not? Why would a man do what he did week after week? Every time God said stand up, he wanted to sit down. Every time God said speak, he said, "What's the use?" He was in a predicament. He didn't want to carry the message but if he tried to be quiet God's word burned in his heart.

Jeremiah wasn't just having a problem with his will, he was having a problem with his perspective. The truth was, and still is, that there was and will always be someone who wants to hear from

God. God reminded me of this one day in a way that I will never forget.

Having been a professional photographer prior to entering the ministry, I decided to help the church raise money by doing family portraits. When the day came, a lady was bringing a young, unchurched boy to have his portrait made. When he inquired where they were going she said, "We're going to the church to have your picture made." "Who's going to make it?" he asked. "The preacher," she responded. "The creature! What's a creature?" he followed up. Laughing, she answered, "Not the creature, the preacher!" "Oh," he said. Then after a pause, he inquired, "What's a preacher?" To her amazement he didn't know what a preacher was. So she tried to think of a simple way to answer him. The answer she came up with was great. "He's someone who tells us about God," she explained. He thought about it for a moment and then said something I'll never forget. He said thoughtfully, "I want him to tell me about God."

When I get discouraged, I think about that little boy and I'm reminded that there is always someone who wants me to tell him about God. That's why I do what I do.

Day 3

CAREFUL WHAT YOU SAY

It's difficult making sense of tragedy, loss and heartache that's the result of an unexpected event in the lives of others as well as in our own. And there is the temptation to try and find some logic or reason for their occurrence. We want to comfort others, but sometimes in our attempt we do so we do more harm than good by our explanations and comments.

When I think about some of the things that I have heard well-meaning people say I cringe. And sometimes it's ministers who say them. I heard about one pastor who was standing at the casket for the final viewing when he observed the daughter of the deceased leaning over her father's body weeping and saying, "O daddy, I can't believe that you're gone. I just can't accept it." To which, for some unknown reason, he reportedly said to her, "Well, you're going to have to accept it, he's gone." Long story made short—she slapped him almost cross-eyed. But now wait. It made sense to him at the time. And that's the problem with speaking before we think. We feel that we must say something, so we just open our mouths and out comes something we wish we could take back.

I've heard of people telling a child, that has had a parent to die, that God "took" the parent or "God must have needed another angel." First of all, we do not become angels when we die; we become glorified saints, which is better. Secondly, God is not in the business of killing mamas and daddies. Even if that's what a person believes the Bible teaches, which I do not, he or she should realize that a child's understanding is limited. Can you imagine how that child will feel toward God believing that God took the parent away from them?

Then there is the statement, "I know how you feel." Think for a moment. Wouldn't you agree that we're all too different and our lives are too different to really know how exactly how someone else feels? If you have indeed been through something similar it is better to say, "I know how it feels to have something like this happen because when it happened to me…" Then relate your experience.

Having been around many difficult situations and having talked with people after the crowds have left; may I offer some suggestions on things that we can say and do to help? We can say, "I'm sorry for your loss." "I'm praying for you." "I love you and if you need me, I'll be there for you." But mostly, when people are hurting they just want to know that you care. Be there for them. Listen. Send a card and write something loving in it—don't just sign it. Send flowers. Take them to lunch and let them talk. Go with them to see their pastor or a qualified counselor. If they are trying to make sense of what's happening, pray for them—but allow them to come up with their own answers. If they are grieving, let them grieve—it's a process through which they must go. Be careful what you say and do and you can be a wonderful blessing to someone.

Day 4

YOU CAN MAKE IT

One of my favorite books is *Children's Letters to God*. On the last page of the book is a letter by a little boy that reads simply, "Dear God, I'm doing the best I can." Signed, Frank. That pretty well says it all sometimes, doesn't it?

I think that I can imagine the little boy's mood and the frustration that he must be feeling. Maybe things haven't been going his way.

He's tried but things just don't seem to work out the way that they should.

Have you felt that way lately? You know, frustrated at life. You've tried and you've prayed but things remain much the same. It kind of makes you want to say, "Lord I'm doing the best I can, why aren't things changing?"

Wouldn't it be nice if God could just send you and me a message in times like these or maybe tell us something encouraging about the future? Well, let's see... I think I read something like that.

Jesus said, "Are not two sparrows sold for a penny? Yet not one of them will fall to the ground apart from the will of your Father. And even the very hairs of your head are all numbered. So don't be afraid; you are worth more than many sparrows." (Matthew 10:29-31) Do you realize what he said? Don't be afraid because you are valuable to Me!

Paul wrote under the inspiration of the Holy Spirit, "If God is for us, who can be against us? He who did not spare his own Son, but gave him up for us all—how will he not also, along with him, graciously give us all things?" (Romans 8:31-32) There are some very important facts here. As a child of God we can rest assured that God alone outnumbers all of our enemies. Secondly, He gave us His own Son, why wouldn't he give us what we need for everyday life?

And later in that chapter Paul continued, "For I am convinced that neither death nor life, neither angels nor demons, neither the present nor the future, nor any powers, neither height nor depth, nor anything else in all creation, will be able to separate us from the love of God that is in Christ Jesus our Lord." (Romans 8:38-9) God and His children are inseparable. No one can come between you and your heavenly Father.

God's word is filled with promises of God's help and encouragement not to give up. Note what we've learned: we are valuable; He provides for us; and no one can separate us from His love. He knows your capabilities and limits; He's not going to let you down if you will trust Him.

As in our own lives, little Frank might have been facing frustrating times but I don't think that he's given up. Notice what he wrote, "Lord, I'm doing the best I can," not "I did the best I could." There's a big difference in those two statements. I believe that little Frank is going to try again tomorrow. What about you?

Day 5

HOW TO MINISTER TO SOMEONE IN NEED

Have you ever wanted to convey something meaningful to someone who is facing difficult times in his/her life but didn't know where to start? There's no way that I can give you the words for every situation; however, I do believe that I can help you to know what direction to take. It seems to me that most people need assurance and want to hear at least three statements in one form or another. First, God loves me. Second, God cares about me. Third, God is going to help me.

Let's look at the first statement, "God loves me." To assume that everyone understands this would be in error. Not everyone understands or even knows the truth of God's word. Still others were taught at some point that God's love is conditional because He's hard and demanding. I know that we shouldn't look at God as if He is some senile old man who will do anything we ask no matter how we live. But at the same time, we must understand that God doesn't divide us into "deserving" and "non-deserving" groups; He will help whoever calls on Him in sincerity. It's important to realize that no one is really going to accept God's help if they are not convinced of His love for them.

Second is the statement, "God cares about me." He doesn't just love me in a warm fuzzy general kind of way; he cares about all that happens to me. The Bible teaches that God is concerned with every aspect of our lives and every need. He's not just some positive force in the universe. For the child of God, He is our closest friend and most faithful ally. Look at it this way—you have many friends but you classify them as friends and close friends. In other words, some care about you on the acquaintance level but some care about you on a personal level. God is on the most intimate and personal level.

Third, "God is going to help me." This is the most difficult statement, not because God might not help, but because it might not be the help people want. We humans, as shortsighted as we are, are convinced that we know what should be done in every situation. This leads us to make demands on God or try to force Him into answering our prayers as we see fit. "Now, Lord if you will just... Then I can..." We think that we know best, but many times we really don't. Personally, I thank God for not answering some of my prayers. There were times I didn't know what I was asking for and, rather than letting me plan my own misfortune, He simply did what was best for me and waited for me to realize that His way was better than mine. It's kind of the way I respond to the unwise request of my children. I'm going to take care of my children—you can count on that—but I'm not always going to let them write the game plan.

I've learned that it is enough to know that in all things he is at work for my good. (Romans 8:28) People need to be reminded of these truths in the time of need and the Bible backs us up all the way.

Day 6

OVERCOMING FEAR

Fear can be a very real adversary. It can be disabling, cause sickness and emotional distress, and thereby disrupt our lives. Fear comes in all different shapes and sizes and varies in intensity from mild to severe.

However, most of the fears we face everyday are not based on facts. They are generated by our feelings. For example, In *Scared to Life* (Victor), Douglas Rumford cites a study conducted by the University of Michigan that explains why we should not allow fear to rule our lives. The study revealed the following: 60% of our fears are totally unwarranted; they never come to pass—20% of our fears are focused on our past, which is completely out of our control—10% of our fears are based on things so petty that they make no difference in our lives—Of the remaining 10%, only 4 to 5% could be considered justifiable.

If we look hard enough, there is enough going on around us to leave us in a perpetual state of fear. But that's not the way the Lord wants us to live. We're not to be bound by fear. But what are we to do when we face anxiety-provoking situations?

Psalm 27 walks us through several steps that the David took in working through his fear—steps that will be helpful in dealing with our own fears.

First of all, we must confront our fears. Many of our fears are in the realm of the unknown and intangible. Too often we allow "what might happen" to plague our minds and consume our thoughts. However, statistics reveal that 95% of the time and energy we spend on fear is completely wasted. If you are always looking for something to be afraid of, it will eventually show up on your doorstep. Remember, our hope lies in the ability of the unbeatable and invincible.

Also, we must understand our reason for our uncertainty. There will always be the temptation to waver in our faith. Everyone experiences uncertainty at times. We often think that certain Christian people are so strong in the Lord that they never have to fight the mental, emotional, and spiritual battles that we do. We see them as mighty warriors who always have it together. But we should realize that those strong people are strong because they rely on God's strength to get them through the battles of life. It's when we deal with our uncertainty and come out on top that we grow in strength and in faith.

Finally, we must embrace our assurance. Assurance is ours because of the consistency of the Lord. God's love is more certain than that of our mother and father. David says, "Though my father and mother forsake me yet the Lord will take care of me." Direction and protection are ours because of God's love. Help is provided for those who wait on the Lord. Someone has said, "God is going to pull you through, if you can stand the pull." Just wait, the Lord will see you through!

If fear concerning a situation or problem is hindering your walk with God, you can turn it all over to Him today. Let me encourage you today to take the steps that David took and you can feel the peace that David felt.

Day 7

SPEAKING OUR MIND

Have you ever met one of those people who would just say whatever came to mind? If it ran through their mind, you could count on it coming out of their mouth. Believe it or not, many of them feel like the woman who confronted C.H. Spurgeon. She told him that her "talent was speaking her mind." He said, "Well, madam, that's one talent the Lord wouldn't mind you burying."

After hurting someone's feelings, I've heard some justify themselves by saying, "The truth will stand when the world's on fire!" As if that makes their hash and critical words OK. Actually, it's the truth of God's word that will stand—not their so-called truth. I imagine theirs will burn if put to the test.

The fact is that the Bible places a great value on being able to hold or control our tongues, not on speaking our mind. Proverbs 15:1-2 tells us, "A gentle answer turns away wrath, but a harsh word stirs up anger. The tongue of the wise commends knowledge, but the mouth of the fool gushes folly." It takes wisdom and self-control to "turn away wrath" anybody can make someone angry. And as for being wise in our speech, an old saying comes to mind. "Better to keep quiet and let people think you're a fool than to open your mouth and remove all doubt."

There's even a strong rebuke for the professing Christian who has no control over his/her tongue. The scripture says, "If anyone considers himself religious and yet does not keep a tight rein on his tongue, he deceives himself and his religion is worthless." (James 1:26)

The scripture gives us some advice on how we can please God with our words. First, let your words be uplifting. Colossians 3:17 says, "And whatever you do, whether in word or deed, do it all in the name of the Lord Jesus, giving thanks to God the Father through him." That narrows down what we can say—doesn't it?

Secondly, let your words be encouraging to others. I Thessalonians 5:14, "And we urge you, brothers, warn those who are idle, encourage the timid, help the weak, be patient with everyone."

Thirdly, let your words show that you are different. James 3:6 says, "The tongue also is a fire, a world of evil among the parts of the body. It corrupts the whole person... (v.9-10) With the tongue we praise our Lord and Father, and with it we curse men, who have been made in God's likeness. Out of the same mouth come praise and cursing. My brothers, this should not be... Who is wise and understanding among you? Let him show it by his good life, by deeds done in the humility that comes from wisdom." (James 3:13)

The best thing we can do is look in the scripture for guidance and pray for the ability to control our words. The next time you are tempted to give someone a piece of your mind, just remember that most of us can't spare any.

Day 8

TOMORROW IS NONE OF OUR BUSINESS

You've probably heard the saying, "Carpe diem," which means, "seize the day!" Nice words, aren't they? Almost makes one feel philosophical to say them. But let's get real. How many of us really try to seize the day? We're too busy worrying and planning for tomorrow. And with good reason, we say. After all, who knows what will happen tomorrow?

The problem is that in our planning for and worrying about tomorrow we never enjoy today. It's a cycle that feeds on itself. Tomorrow we will worry and plan for the next day and so on it goes. Jesus, who has all knowledge and understanding, tried to help us with the right perspective when He said in Matthew 6:34, "Therefore do not worry about tomorrow, for tomorrow will worry about itself. Each day has enough trouble of it's own." He's right, there's enough to be concerned about today without hunting for something in tomorrow.

But there is more. He is speaking to those who believe in God. He wants them to see that people without faith and a belief in God worry about tomorrow—not God's people. He's implying that they should be different.

But wait—that's not all. Note verse 25, "Is not life more important than food, and the body more important than clothes?" He was trying to get them to realize that they had reduced life to surviving. "I've got to have... I need to... "Isn't life about more than surviving? Isn't it about more than what we can collect?" In America we are so materialistic that we are miserable. It seems that everyone wants a piece of the pie but no one has peace of mind. Let's face it, tomorrow scares people.

Corrie Ten Boom said, "Worry does not empty tomorrow of its sorrow, it empties today of its strength." How many of your todays have been ruined by the thought of your tomorrows. The whole idea of the life of faith is that we have enough of the peace of God in our hearts that we can enjoy today without worrying about tomorrow and our strength isn't drained before tomorrow gets here.

Well, what are we supposed to do? Some won't believe me when I tell them, but here goes. We're supposed to trust God with our survival and realize that we have a higher purpose than just surviving. If there is any truth to the Bible then tomorrow is really none of our business—it's God's business.

Sure we're supposed to work and manage our affairs in a responsible manner, but when we place tomorrow in God's hands then we are trusting Him to take care of whatever comes our way, in other words, those things which we cannot manage or foresee. Let me share a theological truth about God that you may not know. God is already in tomorrow waiting for you. He's already at work for you if you are His child. So remember, work on living for today and let God take care of tomorrow.

Day 9

GET RID OF THE GARBAGE

One of my least favorite household chores, to put it mildly, is putting out the garbage. I have to do it the night before, usually when I'm tired. Besides that it's a long walk down the hill to the road. It's a real pain. Can I get an "amen" from the men? But the alternative is worse—you might even say stinks.

I have weaseled out of garbage duty before, convincing my wife that I'll do it next time and that there's not enough garbage to worry about anyway. The cans can hold more. We'll make it to the next pick up day. Well, let me tell you, garbage cans are like baby diapers—they only hold just so much and then look out!

With that in mind, I got to thinking. I'm philosophical you know—at least about garbage. I was thinking about how we allow so much garbage into our minds and how that eventually we pay the price for doing so. So with this in mind, let me tell you about some things that I have learned about garbage and about the human mind.

First, if you don't take out the garbage it begins to pile up. Well that makes sense doesn't it? Why then is it that we are amazed when it happens? "Well," we say, "I meant to but I just forgot about it." I've tried that excuse with my wife. It doesn't work. In the arena of our mind, "garbage thoughts" if you will, seem to multiply when we do not put them out of our mind. In other words, the more negative thoughts we entertain the more they come to us. The more fearful thoughts we allow in our minds the better the selection of terrifying thoughts we have to choose from. The more filth that we dwell on the filthier our thought pattern becomes.

The second profound truth is that, if garbage piles up it's going to start to stink. Has anybody ever been to a sweet smelling landfill? No. And you won't. The reason garbage stinks is that it is rotting. You want to know why some people's attitude stinks—you got it— rotten thoughts. After those negative and nasty thoughts pile up for a while they begin to have an effect on the attitude of the person. We say, "I've had a bad day." "I don't feel good." And we offer many other excuses, some which are true, to justify our rotten attitude. But many times, we must admit, we've let so many negative thoughts pile up that we've developed a rotten attitude.

Third, and trust me on this, if garbage stinks it's going to attract some unwelcome company. Around here it's raccoons that come a-calling. With people and their garbage-filled minds, it's the crowd nobody wants to be around. You know the kind. They are always digging around trying to find something that stinks about someone else so that they can feel superior. It hasn't occurred to them that it's hard to look superior when one's face is in the garbage.

So what's the answer? Get rid of the garbage! Get those garbage thoughts out of your mind and replace them with the right thoughts. For specific counsel get your Bible out and read Philippians 4:8. You'll be glad that you did.

Day 10

WHAT'S YOUR POINT OF VIEW?

Are you one of those people who see the glass half-empty or do you see it half-full? It's an old test that's supposed to identify you as a pessimist or an optimist. Supposedly, the optimist sees the glass half-full—the positive point of view—and the pessimist sees the glass half-empty—the negative point of view. Someone added a third category—the realist. The realist supposedly sees the glass, sees that it is dirty and knows that if she sticks around she will end up washing it!

Whatever your point of view, most would agree that the optimist tends to have the brighter and more encouraging disposition. I believe that I am an optimist—that has to work at it. I want to be perky and bright all the time; but some days I just don't feel perky and bright. "But you're a minister!" some would say. Yes, and I am very much human, too.

With that in mind, let me share with you several "tools" that help me improve my outlook. First, I am a child of God and, "If God be for me who can stand against me?" (Romans 8:31) For me, it all starts here. If it had not been for my conversion, I believe that I would be in jail or in hell. My main reason for having hope for the future is that I know Jesus Christ as my Lord and Savior and I realize that from Him all the blessings of life flow.

Next, I have countless blessings from the Lord. The old song says, "Count your many blessings, name them one by one." Try it sometimes. Stop for a moment and think about or make a list of all the blessing that you have in your life. It's just as easy to think about the good things as it is to gripe and complain; it's simply what one gets used to.

Thirdly, I believe that God honors diligence. In other words, there will always be opportunities for those who will trust God and work hard. I do not believe that I'm striving in vain. God is responding to my calls for help. To be blessed of God, one doesn't have to be the brightest, the most attractive or the best connected—only diligent in living out one's faith. Too many people want the Lord to bless them or to open doors for them without them ever having to lift a finger. But God won't bless laziness. I've worked overtime and extra jobs most of my life, to pay for college, to pay bills and to get ahead in life. And every opportunity to succeed was given to me by God.

There are no perfect situations—there will always be drawbacks. But that doesn't mean that we have to always see the bad. It was Chuck Swindoll that said, "The longer I live the more convinced I become that life is 10 percent what happens to us and 90 percent how we respond to it."

How are you responding to life? What does your outlook say about your attitude? Could your outlook be improved? I believe that through faith and prayer everyone's outlook can be improved. Why not improve your point of view today?

Day 11

THE IMPORTANCE OF HOPE

Many people today face another year, month, or day without hope. They look forward to the future with a blank stare, not knowing what to do or how to respond. Some feel fear, some dread; some feel nothing at all.

It is important to remember that not everyone has a desire to see tomorrow. It is important, because they are the ones to whom we should reaching out. Without hope, a person can become an empty shell and a wandering soul. Without hope there are no dreams and no goals.

"Psychologist William Marston saw this first-hand when he asked three thousand people, 'What have you to live for?' He discovered that 94 percent were simply enduring the present while they waited for the future—waited for something to happen—waited for 'next year' –waited for a 'better time' –waited for 'someone to die' – waited 'for tomorrow.'" In other words, 94% were waiting for hope to come their way; but hope doesn't find us—we must find hope.

Let me point out some of the causes and the best cure for hopelessness. The source of hopelessness, which can often be directly linked to depression, can be physical, situational or even learned behavior. The brain is an organ in our bodies and it can need help just like the other organs of our bodies. Whether it is through doctors or in divine intervention a person who is truly hopeless should seek help of some kind.

Situations or circumstances can leave us feeling hopeless. But situations usually do not last. So don't seek a permanent solution to what is probably a temporary situation.

Then there is the behavior or way of thinking that we have been taught or have adopted. We can learn to be hopeful, just as sure as we can teach ourselves to be hopeless.

This brings me to my personal source of hope. I believe there is hope because I believe the scripture. I base all that I believe about living a hope-filled life on the Bible. Romans 15:4 tells us, "For everything that was written in the past was written to teach us, so that through endurance and the encouragement of the Scriptures we might have hope." Contrary to the ideas of some, the scriptures aren't a list of do's and don'ts. They are encouragement and instruction for us to live our lives to the fullest.

Paul said in Ephesians 1:18. "I pray also that the eyes of your heart may be enlightened in order that you may know the hope to which he has called you." We do not have to live in dread of tomorrow or in hopes that tomorrow will bring us something in which we can hope. We have hope now.

The importance of hope lies in the way in which it affects our outlook. Don't allow hopelessness to blind you to the hope that you have in Jesus Christ. Search the scriptures for encouragement; see the people in the Bible as they are, imperfect, searching and sometimes even unsure about tomorrow. But notice, those who trust in the Lord always find the confidence to go on, no matter what. And you can too.

Day 12

WHAT CAN YOU EXPECT WHEN YOU PRAY?

Prayer is one of those activities that many people think very little about in their busy lives, until there is an urgent need. Sadly, prayer is most often provoked by a sense of need rather than by a desire to communicate with God. Therefore, we often go to God in prayer with urgent expectations about our need. We want to always believe that God will say yes to whatever we ask Him for; but that doesn't always happen. That's right. God doesn't always say yes to our request.

Someone has said that we can always expect God to answer one of three ways: "Yes," "No," or "Wait." The reality is that God can and will say "No." Or He may also tell us to "wait." God is still in charge of answering prayers. So then, what can we expect when we pray?

When our prayer is for a genuine need, we may very well receive the desired answer. By no means am I discouraging anyone from believing for that. However, God does not guarantee that. We may be looking for divine intervention and deliverance—thinking that if we will just have faith we will experience a miraculous deliverance—but then it doesn't happen. Why? Well, I don't know. But I do know that there are many other instances where God did not deliver a person "out" but rather chose to stand with them "through" their trial or time of need. But you will never find a time when God left His people. So whether He says yes or not you can expect God to be with you.

"But if I pray hard enough, will it not change God's mind about helping me?" First, who said He would not help you? Second, the error behind that idea is that we obviously feel that God does not have our best interest at heart. God said in Jeremiah 29:11, "'For I know the plans I have for you'…'plans to prosper you and not to harm you, plans to give you hope and a future.'" God's mind about helping you does not need to be changed. He loves you. You can expect God to have blessings in mind for you.

And do not forget the effect and change that prayer will have on us personally. "Why would prayer change me? The problem is not me! It's that other fellow. Sure, I've got my shortcomings; but if things were different then I wouldn't be like this." But is that the whole truth?

"Well, maybe I could pray a little about myself, my ways and maybe my attitude. Maybe I could spend some time just listening to God, instead of always going down my prayer list like it's a shopping list. Maybe I'll try to do some of the things that God has told me to. Maybe I could deal with life a little better if I had more of a spiritual experience instead of a 'do better' attitude."

When it comes to prayer there are several truths on which we can always depend. First, prayer doesn't always change our situation.

Second, prayer never changes God's mind about us. But, thirdly, prayer always changes us.

Day 13

JESUS DOESN'T WORK ALONE

"Jesus doesn't work alone." Recently I read that statement in an advertisement for a seminary and it struck home with me. What a powerful statement! Many want to know why God does not do more to help people in need. I want to know why we think that God works alone when he has plainly told us in the Bible that he works through us. Paul goes so far as to say that we are "God's fellow workers (1 Corinthians 3:9)."

In Matthew 25:35-40 we have a memorable passage that impresses on us how important God considers our response to the needs of our fellow man. Now, before anyone misses the point, remember that it is not our response to the needs of others that will save us or make us a Christian; but it is our response by which we will be judged.

Notice that when Christ judges man he will say to those who have been compassionate followers of his, "For I was hungry and you gave me something to eat, I was thirsty and you gave me something to drink, I was a stranger and you invited me in, I needed clothes and you clothed me, I was sick and you looked after me, I was in prison and you came to visit me.' 'Then the righteous will answer him, 'Lord, when did we see you hungry and feed you, or thirsty and give you something to drink? When did we see you a stranger and invite you in, or needing clothes and clothe you? When did we see you sick or in prison and go to visit you?' 'The King will reply, 'I tell you the truth, whatever you did for one of the least of these brothers of mine, you did for me.'" NIV

Read on and you will find out what happens to those who failed to follow God and who failed to respond to the needs at hand. The Lord takes our service to others or lack of, very personally. Even John had some strong words on the subject, "If anyone has material possessions and sees his brother in need but has no pity on him, how can the love of God be in him? (I John 3:17)." NIV

I read the story of a little boy who had become a Christian through a mission in the inner city slums of a large city. Of course the little boy was poor and in great need, but he was also bright and enthusiastic about his new faith. One day after his newfound conversion, a mean spirited and unbelieving man he encountered began to taunt him about his faith in God. The man said to the little boy, "If God really loves you, why doesn't he tell someone to buy you a new pair of shoes to replace those old things you're wearing? And why doesn't he tell someone to buy you some new clothes or some decent food? "Well," the man said, "tell me!" The ragged little boy, refusing to doubt God, thought for a moment and then replied, "Maybe he did tell somebody; but maybe somebody forgot."

Somebody did forget. And I know what they forgot. They forgot that Jesus doesn't work alone.

Day 14

THE IMPORTANCE OF REST

Not long ago I read the heartbreaking story of lawyer in San Antonio Texas. It happened several years ago but then again it might have happened again to someone else just yesterday. According to the newspaper report, this young, newly married, up-and-coming lawyer came home from work one day, took a gun from his safe, crawled into a sleeping bag and shot himself. He left a note for his new bride that read simply, "It's not that I don't love you, but I'm so tired and I've got to rest."

I wonder how many more people are out there who feel the same way. They may have plenty materially, they may have nothing; but they want the same thing—rest. Just living in this world can leave us feeling pushed and pressured above our ability to cope. Computers were supposed to make our lives so simple that we would live in a world with more leisure time than ever before. But these and other so-called time saving devices were never the answer to our problem of weariness. Weariness of mind is usually not the result of the hours we put in at the workplace—it is that somehow life keeps getting more complicated?

Medication may relax us but it gives us no assurance about tomorrow. We can medicate ourselves into a stupor or get so high that everything seems wonderful. But tomorrow is coming and what will we do then?

Positive thinking may change our outlook, but there are still situations beyond our control. I believe in having a positive attitude, but that does not always make it possible for me to change life's circumstances. My only true hope and rest lies with Jesus Christ. He offers help to the weary and burdened when He says, "Come to me, all you who are weary and burdened, and I will give you rest. Take my yoke upon you and learn from me, for I am gentle and humble in heart, and you will find rest for your souls. For my yoke is easy and my burden is light." Matthew 11:28-30 NIV In this passage, He used a familiar farming illustration for the people that would relate to them the need for them to trade their unbearable burden for one that was lighter. This is where we see the importance of receiving rest; for without rest, the heaviness remains and continues to press down upon us.

When we come to Him He takes over. I understand the theology of it but for the life of me I cannot tell you how He does it. What I can tell you, is that I found rest when I came to Him. There is an old song that says, in part, "At the cross, at the cross where I first saw the light, and the burdens of my heart rolled away, it was there by faith, that I received my sight and now I am happy all the day." Those words aptly explain my experience.

I know that may sound old-fashioned to some, but the rest I feel right now, well, I would not trade it for the world. There are all kinds of help for those who need rest, but there is none that is as sweet as the rest that I have found in Jesus.

Day 15

NOT JUST FORGIVEN

Have you ever seen the bumper sticker or heard the expression that states, "Christians are not perfect, just forgiven"? The point is to convey the message to the critics that seek to point out every flaw, failure or sin in the lives of Christian people that being a Christian does not make a person perfect. Having a desire and a commitment to avoid or abstain from sin does not mean the goal is always achieved.

However, too many Christians have taken the statement, "I am not perfect, just forgiven," to extremes and made it the ruling philosophy of their lives—instead of basing their outlook on the Word of God. The problem is that, although being a Christian is based on God's willingness to forgive us and not on our perfection, "just forgiven" is not much to celebrate nor is it the whole story.

Think for a moment. What kind of life is "just forgiven." Is that all there is to a Christian experience? Not if you read the Bible. Look at 2 Corinthians 5:17: "Therefore, if anyone is in Christ, he is a new creation; the old has gone, the new has come!" Read all of Romans chapter 6 but be sure and note the theme found, in part, in verse four: "We were therefore buried with him through baptism into death in order that, just as Christ was raised from the dead through the glory of the Father, we too may live a new life." NIV

People often speak of being "empowered" by a lifestyle change, a new position in life or by newly acquired wealth or knowledge. But if anyone has the right to feel empowered, it is those who have trusted in the truth of God's Word and the new life that Jesus Christ makes possible. Paul wrote, "Do not conform any longer to the pattern of this world, but be transformed by the renewing of your mind." NIV To say that just being forgiven is the best we can hope for is to miss the great truth of scripture. We can be transformed— even if it is little by little. It is this knowledge that empowers us to live for Christ in the first place.

No, I am not perfect, but neither am I "just forgiven." I am transformed, I am liberated and I am loved with an everlasting love. I am different than I was before, I am hopeful and believing. I do not fear tomorrow and I do not dread the future. I do not hate my brother, I am not lost but I have been found and, yes, "I was blind but now I see."

The past is behind me and my future awaits me. Earth may be my home but heaven is my destiny. I am what I am and have what I have all by the grace of God. I may have faults and failures and I may be imperfect. But one thing is for sure—I am not "just forgiven."

Day 16

FORGOTTEN THANK YOU'S

At times I forget things. In fact, like someone said, at the rate I am going it will not be long until I can hide my own Easter eggs. We all forget things from time to time—some are really not important, but then some are.

Saying "thank you" is something important that all of us tend to forget from time to time. In particular, we forget to say thanks to the people in our lives that help us or bless us in one way or another. If we are honest we can all remember some forgotten "thank you's" that need to be given to those who have touched our lives.

When I think of the people that I have forgotten to thank, two people immediately come to mind—one I haven't seen for years. Her name is Kay Jones. She was my quiet, unassuming childhood Sunday school teacher. I was not her best student by a long shot, nor did I attend very regularly. But I remember that once when I was sick she sent me a card and a box of candy. She would often send me cards and ask about me when I was absent. In all honesty, Kay, I do not remember anything you said in class, but I remember what you did and I always believed that you loved me. That means a great deal to a child. I am late, but thank you.

Then there was this guy I worked with several years ago. His name is David Moon and he was a good friend. Though I did not realize it then, I know now what David did for me. He discipled me in the early years of my faith. He is not a pastor or a preacher but he taught me a great number of things about being a Christian. He would make me think about what I believed. Boy, was that annoying! I wanted everything to be about the way I felt. I wanted to educate everyone with my opinion. I did not want to think; I knew everything. I had to have been a pain. But David was patient. Day in and day out he offered me his friendship, his acceptance and many challenging questions about my faith that, in time, made me stronger and more understanding of others. I can still hear him in my words when I deliver a sermon. I am a little late, but thank you.

I also had a New Testament professor that taught us that thank you notes were scriptural. He then cited all the places in the New Testament where Paul and others made a point to thank someone for something done or for a gift received. Thanks Dr. Trucks.

With this in mind, to whom do you owe a thank you for a kind word or deed? Is it a relative, a friend, a teacher, a minister, maybe it is your mom or dad? Pick up the phone and call them right now or send that card that you have been meaning to send. Do not do it tomorrow. Do it today. Just say, "By the way, I forgot to say thank you for what you did." You will be glad that you did and they will be, too.

Wait! I almost forgot the most important thank you of all. When is the last time you told God thank you? You don't need a card or a phone to do that.

Day 17

DEALING WITH DEATH'S TRAGEDY

I was in the check out line the other day when a woman approached the checkout with a large floral arrangement and several small children in tow. As I stood there I overheard one of the little girls ask what the flowers were for. The woman responded that they were for the grave of someone (a lady she called by name, presumably a relative) who had recently died. "Remember she died not too long ago." The lady said to the child. "How did she die?" the girl asked. The woman responded, "She was killed in a car accident." It was then that many of the past tragedies that I have witnessed were brought to mind. Parents, children, friends—some older, some younger—but all people cut down in the prime of life. I do not have the wisdom, knowledge or space to explain the "why" of it all. Even the very idea of offering words, seems at best, an inadequate offering. But I can suggest some ways that we might be able to deal with such tragedies.

We must grieve, but not as those who are without hope. The scriptures never forbid us to grieve. It is human and natural to grieve. But Paul said, "Do not grieve as those who have no hope." What is our hope? Remember King David? After his infant son died he said in essence, "He cannot come back to me but I can go to him." (2 Samuel 12:23) He was speaking of that future reunion that he would have with his child. That hope.

Next, we must continue on, but not as if we have forgotten. I have always said that one of the saddest aspects of death is that life goes on. Life must go on and we must go on as well. But we can remember and cherish what we had with the person we lost.

And we look to the future with confidence and faith. We know that we cannot live in the past. Nor can we hide away in our home refusing to live out our own life. There is too much to live for. Those whom we have loved and who have loved us would want us to live our life to the fullest. To live on is a critical choice that we have to make. Remember what Jesus said in John 10:10. "The thief comes only to steal and kill and destroy; I have come that they may have life, and have it to the full." NIV

Do not allow yourself to be robbed of life. Jesus promises that He will lead you into a full life if you will follow Him. God wants you to have a good life. Your loved one would want you to have a good life.

Do what you must to deal with your grief. Pray. Do not deny your feelings. Do not hide away forever. Seek counseling if you want—but live on.

The girl in the store asked one more question that stirred me. She asked, "Did she die again?" "No," the woman responded. No, I thought, there is no reason to die twice as long as we know Jesus. I couldn't help but think of what John said in Revelation 20:6, "Blessed and holy are those who have part in the first resurrection. The second death has no power over them." NIV Make your peace and move forward.

Day 18

TAKE HEART IN TIMES OF TROUBLE

I heard the story of a rancher out west who went to check on his cattle and hired hands. As he topped a hill he looked down in the little valley to see one of his ranch hands, which must have fallen off his horse, running from a large bull. Just as the bull was about to catch up with him, the cowboy jumped into a large hole. The bull barely missed him and ran on by. But no sooner had the cowboy gotten safely in the hole until he jumped out again. To the amazement of the rancher this happened several more times. Every time the cowboy would escape the attack of the bull by jumping in the hole, he would immediately jump out again. Finally the rancher called down to the cowboy, "Why don't you just stay in the hole!" To which the cowboy yelled back, while on the run, "There's a bear in the hole!"

Have you ever felt that way—you know—between the bear and the bull with no where to hide? Sometimes it would seem that there is no place to hide and no situation that makes us feel safe. What we need is a refuge.

David wrote in Psalms 31:1-4, "In you Lord I have taken refuge." Webster's defines refuge as, "Shelter or protection from danger or difficulty." Also, "A person or thing that gives shelter, help or comfort." David needed it all.

David needed refuge from his own personal storm. Note the characteristics of his storm: distress, sorrow, grief, anguish, affliction and, to top it all off, he had been forsaken by his friends and felt that he was forgotten. I think that is enough troubles for one day.

Now do you understand why he needed a refuge? I imagine that someone reading this can identify with his feelings. It is not that you think that you can run from life, but right now all you want is a place to hide—a shelter from the storm. You are between the bear and the bull, so to speak, and you are getting tired. Don't lose hope.

I know that David did not lose hope because of the word he used in verse 22—"yet." That is a big word when it appears that your troubles are about to overcome you. He said, "Yet you heard my cry for mercy when I called to you for help." NIV He had called for help and the Lord had heard him. He knew that he could trust the Lord in times of difficulty. In fact he said, "In you I put my trust (v.1), and I trust in you (v.14).

It is noteworthy to mention that refuge exists whether anyone takes advantage of it or not. Often our struggle lies with trusting in the refuge; not whether or not there is a refuge. We know, or at least feel, that God is there; it is just that we are unsure of how much we can trust Him with. But David had a history with God. He had learned to trust Him—maybe little by little—but he learned. And when the storm came he knew where to turn.

Let me leave you with the words of a man who knew what to do in times of trouble, "Be strong and take heart, all you who hope in the LORD (v.24)."

Day 19

THE POISON OF BITTERNESS

Who was it that hurt you? Did a face or name immediately come to mind? I did not have ask when or how or when did I? Emotional hurts heal slowly, often leaving behind anything from a residue of resentment to a deep bruise filled with bitterness. Allowing the past to remain in the past is easier said than done.

What we must strive to do when dealing with past hurts is to just let them go. Unconsciously, I think we hold onto hurts even though we realize that we must let them go and we sincerely want to put them behind us. That is why, at times, we must make a conscious effort to release the hurt and the person who hurt us. But how? That is the question.

First we must refuse to rehearse the event. I have been in enough church plays and cantatas to know that if I do not want to forget my lines or the words to the song, then I will have to rehearse my part.

Have you ever rehearsed something so much that you woke in the middle of the night with your part or the answers to the test running through your mind?

Now think about this. When you and I spend our time thinking about the hurts others have caused us, is it any wonder that we cannot get them off our mind? The hurt is burned into our minds through repetitious thinking.

Secondly, we must refuse to discuss the outcome. Often, people who have been hurt find themselves keeping score or a record in their mind of how much the other person has gotten away with in relation to themselves. When they see the person who hurt them and they seem to be doing well, it just adds insult to injury. We want the outcome to be in our favor. If it is not, it seems to make the injury suffered worse. Do not keep score. Do not even think about the outcome. It will do you no good. Let God settle the account. (Romans 12:19)

Thirdly, we must let it die. Sometimes our past injuries take on a life of their own. I have met people, who, if they did not have their hurts, they would have nothing at all. Their whole life centered on their hurts. It is what they thought about and talked about all the time. Their wounds were like their trophies; their heartache was their badge of honor. I have noticed one other thing about them— others often avoided them. No one wants to stay around a bitter person, except another bitter person. Misery loves company.

If we only pay lip service to the act of letting go, that old hurt will return quickly and begin to thrive with new life. We must cut off the life-giving resources that feed it. When we do, it will cease to drain us and it will die.

It would be best for me to leave you with the wisdom of the scripture on this matter. Paul wrote, "Get rid of all bitterness, rage and anger, brawling and slander, along with every form of malice. Be kind and compassionate to one another, forgiving each other, just as in Christ God forgave you." Ephesians 4:31-32 NIV

Day 20

FORGIVENESS: DOES IT REALLY WORK?

We talk about forgiveness. We want forgiveness. We believe strongly in the philosophy of forgiveness. But too many fail to practice forgiveness. That is why I must tell you that sometimes forgiveness appears not to work. I say "appears" because if we observe the actions of some, we might get the idea that forgiveness is an occasional solution that can be employed if desired.

Forgiveness will only work if it is seen as a necessary act. As long as we can devise another plan of action other than going through with the act of forgiving, forgiveness will not work. By our unwillingness to forgive we render the entire solution powerless. Forgiveness that has not been offered is as powerless as an untouched light switch in a dark room. Knowing that it is there does not remove the darkness. It is only when we flip the switch that the darkness is eliminated. When we see the necessity of forgiveness and act on it, the switch is flipped and the darkness is dispelled. Refusing to forgive, however, is like remaining in the darkness.

Forgiveness will only work if it is something that we really want. You know the old saying, "You can lead a horse to water, but you cannot make him drink." Well, if you and I do not want to forgive someone, it will not take place. Now, that is as simple as it can get. The point I want us to see is that we must take personal responsibility for forgiving someone. Do not use those worn out excuses; we can forgive if we want to.

Forgiveness will only work if it is something we can live with. What I mean is, forgiveness will work if we will forgive and then leave the issue and decision alone. Stop wrestling with it, stop analyzing it, stop looking for a reason to take it back from the person you gave it to. You have made your decision to forgive, if for no other reason for yourself, and now you're going to live with that decision.

Forgiveness is an action word. Although it is often yoked with the word forgetfulness, forgiveness does not make us forget. Forgiveness overcomes the memory of the wrong done and it chooses to treat the individual as if he had never done anything wrong. And right there is the problem. We just do not want to treat someone who did us wrong as though they were innocent of all charges. I think we feel a sense of power over them when we refuse to let them forget their actions. We like to think that we can make them suffer for their wrong as long as we hold it over their head.

And all the time, we are forgetting that we have been asking God to forgive us of our wrongs, yet we will not do the same. Jesus gets right to the point when He says in Matthew 6:15, "If you do not forgive men their sins, your Father will not forgive your sins." Forgiveness will work if we will commit ourselves to giving it.

Day 21

KEEP MOVING FORWARD

Doesn't it seem that sometimes it would be easier to give up than to keep pressing on against the odds? Many have felt that way or at least they have felt the fatigue of trying to live a life of quality and character in the face of so much in life that wants to derail us from our purpose. Even those who will devote their lives to following God and fulfilling His will, will become tired at times. Life is not always easy—even when lived for God.

The apostle Paul is a man we know from the Bible who most Christians think of as a spiritual superman, and yet he was a man who had suffered a great number of adversities and trials in his quest to follow God. In addition, he knew that he was no superman. He knew his strength was in Christ. That is why he wrote, "I can do everything through him who gives me strength." Philippians 4:13 NIV He knew that he could make it, but only through the strength that comes from God.

Even with that strength, in his letter to the Philippian church, he used the term "pressing" to describe his forward progress. He was pushing himself toward his goal of becoming all that God wanted him to be. He writes, "Not that I have already obtained all this, or have already been made perfect, but I press on to take hold of that for which Christ Jesus took hold of me." Philippians 3:12 NIV Most all things that are worthwhile do not come easy.

He was saying, "I am trying with all that is within me to live the life that Christ meant for me to live." Many have wanted that same thing, but all have faced obstacles. And it is those obstacles that get us down at times. Too many obstacles can zap one's strength. Too many obstacles can make anyone want to give up. But you and I know that we cannot give up no matter how many obstacles we face. We must determine that by His help and strength we will make it through anything that comes our way.

Someone wrote a little poem with which I would like to leave you.

> Two frogs fell into a deep cream bowl,
> One was an optimistic soul
> But the other took the gloomy view,
> "I shall drown," he cried, "and so will you."
> So with a last despairing cry,

He closed his eyes and said, "Good-bye."
But the other frog, with a merry grin,
Said, "I can't get out, but I won't give in!
I'll swim around till my strength is spent.
For having tried, I'll die content."
Bravely he swam until it would seem
His struggles began to churn the cream.
On the top of the butter at last he stopped
And out of the bowl he happily hopped.
What is the moral? It's easily found.
If you can't get out—keep swimming around!

Day 22

THE PROBLEM WITH CRITICS

Do you not just love a critic? No, I am not serious. Critics are annoying to say the least. The main problem with critics is that they are everywhere. You may live with one. You may even work with one or for one. They are on the radio, television, in newspapers and magazines. We do not seem to be able to get away from them. But what do we do with them?

The best answer that I can think of is to ignore the critic. That is really all that we can do. Do not try arguing with them; it only gives them the opportunity to make their case for whatever negative point of view that they hold. Many critics are only looking for a forum anyway. Give them the floor and they will drone on endlessly about the problems with people, religion, politics, the government, society, education, etc. But rarely do they offer a solution.

In short, I think that I can sum up their point of view. If you are for it, they are against it. If you think that it will work, they will say that it will not. If you say try, they say what is the use. They must think that most people are too stupid or ill informed to do their jobs, make proper choices, or even live their lives. Why do they think this way? Apparently, they seem to think that they have the correct point of view or understanding on everything and rarely do they need to change their mind. Their function in life is to point out the errors of others and of society. That is how they help us. Yeah, right.

Therefore, live your life with the determination to succeed in the face of those who will argue that you cannot. Chart your own course with the guidance and direction that you receive from God's Word and the Holy Spirit. Recognize that God wants you to be blessed and that if you follow His directions you will succeed. Say as James advised, "If it is the Lord's will, we will live and do this or that." James 4:15 NIV And having your course charted with God's blessings, set off toward your goal.

But remember, there will be critics all along the way; you must maintain your focus. In his book, *He Still Moves Stones*, Max Lucado gives us some excellent advice for dealing with critics. He writes, "Ignore what people say. Block them out. Turn them off. Close your ears. And, if you have to, walk away.

Ignore the ones who say it's too late to start over. Disregard those who say you'll never amount to anything. Turn a deaf ear toward those who say that you aren't smart enough, fast enough, tall enough, or big enough—ignore them. Faith sometimes begins by stuffing your ears with cotton."

The problem with critics is, well, that they are always critical and negative. Just be sure that their problem does not become yours.

Day 23

OUR ACTIONS MATTER

What good is religion if there is no transformation of one's life for the better? I cannot speak to all other religions, but I can tell you that true Christianity is a religion that goes beyond the mind or the intellect to affect the behavior and actions of the individual. Anything short of that is substandard and not what the scripture teaches.

I realize that some may not stress the importance of our behavior—making Christianity only a matter of the heart. Some may overemphasize it to the point of reducing Christianity to merely good moral behavior. However one truth remains, faith lived out because of a transformed heart is the only faith that is real. But do not take my word for it; let us go beyond my opinion to the scriptures.

Concerning our acts of charity and compassion, "This is how we know what love is: Jesus Christ laid down his life for us. And we ought to lay down our lives for our brothers. If anyone has material possessions and sees his brother in need but has no pity on him, how can the love of God be in him? Dear children, let us not love with words or tongue but with actions and in truth." I John 3:16-18 NIV

Concerning pleasing God, "Religion that God our Father accepts as pure and faultless is this: to look after orphans and widows in their distress and to keep oneself from being polluted by the world." James 1:27 NIV

Concerning our reactions to others, "Make sure that nobody pays back wrong for wrong, but always try to be kind to each other and to everyone else." I Thess.5:15 NIV   And concerning unity and love, "Carry each other's burdens, and in this way you will fulfill the law of Christ." Gal. 6:2 NIV

These are just a sampling of instructions given to us by God concerning our behavior.   They are just the tip of the proverbial iceberg. Now remember, they and the others were not given for us to use as a rule book but rather as a yard stick by which we can measure our own lives after the fact.   The true essence of a real godly experience is that it comes from the heart. The Word of God simply keeps it from being so subjective.

Will I please everyone if I do this?   Will everyone think very highly of me? I cannot guarantee that. People can be very unfair and uninformed in their judgments. And some base their opinion on whether or not you please them or do what they want. All I can tell you is that I believe that the essence of true Christianity is a life that resembles the life Jesus lived.

Ultimately, the final judgment of our life will be rendered by God and not by man.   But in no wise does that free us from the responsibility and obligation to live a life that benefits, not only ourselves, but also others. The way we live our lives really does matter.

Day 24

WHOM CAN WE TRUST?

Whom do you trust? I mean really trust? If you are like many Americans, your list is not too long. We seem to live in a cynical and jaded society that tends to expect the worst out of people instead of the best. According to a statistic quoted in *Harper's* magazine 4/96 issue, the percentage of Americans who believe that "most people can be trusted" is only 35 percent.

Why is it that so many people seem to be unwilling to trust another person?   We could talk about crime, scams and crooked people all day. But more specifically, why do we not seem to trust the people that we often associate with and to whom we are related? The crooked group we do not trust mainly out of fear. But the second group we may tend to mistrust because we feel that they have failed us.

It is difficult for trust and confidence to be restored to a relationship once it is lost. Most often, the reason for losing trust in another has to do with the fact that we were deceived, let down or betrayed. And certainly, it is not in our best interest to be too quick to place our trust in someone who has repeatedly failed us. We would think ourselves gullible if we did that. So before we know it we are stuck—we trust no one. The problem with that is that we become more and more insecure and defensive. And we all know that everyone wants to associate with an insecure and defensive person—not quite. So what are we to do? There are a few suggestions I can offer when trust or lack of trust becomes a problem.

First, if another chance can be given to someone without endangering you or someone else's welfare, do so. Sure, you could get hurt emotionally; that is a possibility. But then again, you could win a friend or restore a family's unity. Start off small, be willing to give a little, hope a little and love a little. The faith you place in that "someone" will be a great encouragement to them.

If trust cannot be restored in a relationship, and you have tried, be wise—it is not your failure. Simply put, some people have no right to ask others to trust them. From this point it is their responsibility to rebuild their integrity and reputation. Jesus Christ never tells us to be foolish in our relationships with others.

And most importantly, to keep all things in perspective, place your trust in the Lord. Proverbs 3:5-6, "Trust in the LORD with all your heart and lean not on your own understanding; in all your ways acknowledge him, and he will make your paths straight." Too much of life lies in the realm of the unseen for us to ever have complete peace about a difficult relationship or a situation without His assurance. Emerson wrote, "All I have seen teaches me to trust the Creator for all I have not seen." In short, I think that life tells us that we need God. And in return, God tells us that we can depend on Him even if we can depend on no other

Day 25

ARE YOU A SUCCESS?

Do you remember the commercial where several men are working out in a weight room and an announcement comes over the intercom, "The driver of the tan minivan, you have left your lights on"? They all glance around at one another, but the driver of the minivan does not want to move because he is embarrassed that he drives a tan minivan. Then, a really manly, shiny and expensive vehicle is presented.

Sadly, this is an effective ad in America. But think about it, if the vehicle that we drive, the house in which we live and the clothes which we wear are the things that make us feel successful, we are in sad shape. In our society, the methods and measurements of success are promoted and packaged by people who have "been there and done that" and want you to be a success, too! It is not that following their advice in certain arenas would hurt. But some goals and levels of success are easily measured—some are not.

What about those things that are not so easily measured? What about a life of true public service, where there are no "perks" or big money, just helping people? What about the nameless moms and dads who reared the great leaders and productive citizens of our nation? What about the caregiver who has spent the most productive years of her life caring for dying family members for no pay and virtually no recognition? How do we measure their success? After all, they probably drive a tan minivan.

As a minister and a Christian, I have struggled with the idea of success. In the past, success was easier to define. But now I am aware that my work and life are not so easy to measure in terms of success and failure; things have changed. I still very much want to succeed. I believe that God wants me to succeed. I just cannot measure my success in most areas by any standard of our society. The apostle Paul said it this way, "Do not conform any longer to the pattern of this world, but be transformed by the renewing of your mind. Then you will be able to test and approve what God's will is— his good, pleasing and perfect will." Romans 12:2 NIV

I cannot tell you if everyone will judge you and me as successes or not, but what does it matter as long as you and I please God? If we please God, we will be honest, trustworthy, kind, considerate, faithful and loving; we will be builders of a better world, not destroyers of our present world.

In John Maxwell's book, *The 21 Irrefutable Laws of Leadership*, he wrote, "A leader always finds a way to win." Challenged by the statement, I determined that I was going to find a way to win in every situation—I was always going to be successful no matter what. Well, the problem is that most of the successes of our lives cannot be plotted on a graph or displayed on a chart. Besides, the measurement of success tends to be so subjective and superficial.

Therefore, I have returned to the only standard that is constant, attainable and meaningful—God's word. I have found "a way to win." I will do the best I can in every endeavor and I will be faithful to all that I have committed myself. If that does not make me a success, nothing else will.

Day 26

OVERCOMING LONELINESS

The sensation of being alone can be very real and troubling. Often this feeling comes upon us when we are in a time of despair, heartache, trouble or a time of decision. But for many more it is an abiding sensation that cannot be shaken.

There are multitudes in the world today who feel that no one really cares for them. They face the world with a smile so that no one will see the pain that they are going through. We often think that we can sense what people are feeling, but often times we are wrong. We may think that we are the only ones who feel lonely at times and we are wrong again. With this in mind there are several misconceptions that I would like to deal with concerning loneliness.

First, there is the idea that "If I am socially involved I will never be lonely." Many people want relationships but cannot seem to fit them into their schedule. They are amazed that they are around so many people and yet have no real friends. But we must remember that friendships are built through investing time in another person, not through social involvement. Though sometimes consuming, it is individual relationships that we need.

Next, "If I am self-sufficient I will never be lonely." Many see self-sufficiency as the cure all for self-image problems. Some simply refuse to admit that they need someone else. Some do not want to get hurt. Whatever the case, no matter how independent that one may become, he or she will always need a friend.

And thirdly, "If I feel lonely it is because God has forsaken me."

Many have wondered, "If God were near wouldn't I feel His presence?" I believe that we can feel the presence of God. But do not rely on feeling alone. Too often we see God as being distant and disconnected from our lives. We're like the little boy who had problems repeating the Lord's prayer. He prayed, "Our father, who art in heaven, how'd you know my name?" We doubt God because we have not gotten to know Him. However, David, a man who knew God, wrote in Psalms 139, "You have hedged me behind and before, And laid your hand upon me. Such knowledge is too wonderful for me; It is high, I cannot attain it. Where can I go from your Spirit? Or where can I flee from your presence? If I ascend into heaven, you are there; If I make my bed in hell, behold you are there." NKJV

As we can see, these and many more misconceptions about loneliness have caused many to be distraught for long periods of time when they could have looked to the Lord and found hope and looked to others and found friendship.

How do I make friends? We must show ourselves friendly. How do I avoid disappointment with people? Keep your eyes on the Lord. How can I know that God has not left me alone? Trust in His word.

Day 27

DARE TO CHANGE

If all my experiences with people have taught me one thing, it is that most people do not like change. Mark Twain said, "The only person who likes change is a wet baby." Well, that is about right from what I have experienced. In most cases people wish to remain as they are—maybe it is human nature, maybe it is our own insecurities, maybe we do not see the need or maybe we just like things the way that they are. As we enter the New Year, let us just think about change and the good that it might do us. But where do we start?

The best place to start is with ourselves. Sometimes making changes in our own life does away with the need to change other people and situations. What is it that we can change about our attitude, actions and activities that will help us to be a more pleasing and productive person?

To begin with, attitude directly impacts our lives and the lives of those around us more than anything else. Attitude will determine our reaction to most events that take place in our lives. If our attitude is one which always leads us to see ourselves as victims or failures, then we will tend to immediately respond in a very negative way when adversity comes. All problems will tend to be seen as an attack us or as God out to get us. We must stop believing that we are doomed and rejected and start believing that we are valuable and profitable.

We must be willing to take responsibility for our actions. Our actions are our own and not something that someone else made us do. Some Christians that I have dealt with seem to have what I call "Flip Wilson theology." If you remember, Flip Wilson was a comedian in the 70's who had a famous line that he used, "The devil made me do it." Some want to think that it is always someone else's fault that they behaved the way that they did—either the devil or someone else. If we are to change we must not consider what other will do but what will I choose to do.

Our activities are important as well. The activities that we engage in will always have an impact on our lives. Something as simple as exercise can completely change the way we feel physically and emotionally. Uplifting entertainment will give us the break we need from the routine of life. Participation in worthwhile activities such as helping someone else, civic involvement and weekly worship will help us remember that the world does not revolve around us.

Making the changes in our own lives will not only keep us busy for a while, but will also set us free from trying to change those around us. Which, by the way, is not going to happen anyway. Situations and circumstances will not impact us as much and we will face tomorrow with a brighter outlook. If we dare to make the changes, we will reap the blessings. (Mt 18:1-4; Eph. 4:21-24; Phil. 2:5-15)

Day 28

IT'S EASY TO TALK ABOUT LOVE

Last night as I put my daughter to bed I told her, as I always do, that I loved her. She responded in kind by saying, "I love you, too, daddy." Then she said, "I love everybody in the whole world." "You do?" I asked. "Yea. Do you daddy?" There it was. One of those questions that children ask that takes a parent off guard. I could have just responded by saying, "Yes, honey, now go to sleep." But I could not say it.

No, I do not feel hatred toward anyone and no I am not angry with anyone. It just would not have been a completely honest answer. So I answered the best I could. I said, "I try to love everybody." O.K., so maybe that was not the best answer to give. But the problem is that she is only four years old and she does not know that there are people in the world who are very difficult to love because of their actions and words. In her world everybody seems to love her and her greatest injustice is being pushed at recess. But I have seen how vicious and cruel that some people can be in this world and that is where my difficulty arises.

I am aware that as a Christian that I am supposed to have love for everyone and I do try to care about everyone. But too often when we talk about love we are talking more about feelings more so than about the reality of living everyday in this world. The reality is that we see so much everyday and experience so much in a lifetime that it makes it difficult to really show love to everyone.

For a child who has not been mistreated, it may be easier to love everybody because she may not see the faults of others, the wrongs and the meanness that they do. They may not understand motives and actions as we adults do. The innocence of a child is wonderful when it comes to loving. I do not think that we as adults are going to get our innocence back, but we can find love in our hearts just the same.

We can start by caring. Loving people can become a habit just like hating or not trusting people can. If we make a habit of seeing the best in people and expressing our love toward people, it will become second nature.

Focusing on the need of the person that we are having difficulty loving might enable us to see past their behavior. Sometimes there is a need in a person's life that is causing them to behave as they do. Sometimes adults do what children do—they act out to get attention. And for some, any attention is better than none.

When I told my daughter that not everybody in the world treats people right, she said, "Yea, at school there is a boy who is mean to everybody." To which I responded that maybe he just needed Jesus in his heart. "Yea," she said. "Maybe we should just pray that he would get Jesus in his heart." "Yea," she said, "we will pray that he gets Jesus in his heart."

I thought later that we all need to make sure that we have Jesus in our hearts because it is much easier to talk about loving everybody than to actually do it.

Day 29

THE PROBLEM WITH JUDGING OTHERS

Have you ever had someone make an unfair and inaccurate assumption about your intentions or your feelings? I suppose that we all have had that to happen. Most of the time people are completely wrong in their assumptions; but even if they were not, they are still on dangerous ground because of what the scripture says. "Do not judge, or you too will be judged. For in the same way you judge others, you will be judged, and with the measure you use, it will be measured to you." Matthew 7:1-2

Let me be specific as to what it means to judge another. Judging is the willingness to accept rumor as fact. Judging is the practice of beating another over the head with their mistakes. It is the assumption that a person is guilty without any concrete evidence to convict them. Judging is the act of a critic – not a Christian. It comes from the heart of a cynic—not a child of God.

I will agree that we may be able to tell if someone's actions are right or wrong, but to go as far as to say that we know what is in the heart is to go too far; yet that is the essence of judging. When we judge another we are making a couple of dangerous assumptions.

First, we assume that we have the right to judge someone because of the estimation of our own self. We are assuming that we are superior to the person that we judge. This is the basis of hatred and prejudice. Of Jesus, who had every right to judge us all and lord His righteousness over others, Paul wrote, "Your attitude should be the same as that of Christ Jesus: Who, being in very nature God, did not consider equality with God something to be grasped, but made himself nothing, taking the very nature of a servant, being made in human likeness. And being found in appearance as a man, he humbled himself and became obedient to death—even death on a cross!" Philippians 2:5-8 NIV Jesus—who knows the very thoughts and intents of every heart—was willing to die for us all. That does not sound like someone who is elevating Himself above others. To put it plainly, if we are going to have His attitude we had better get off our "high horse."

Secondly, we wrongly assume that we are qualified to serve as another's judge. The problem with some people seems to be that they cannot possibly see that they have the same potential to be wrong themselves. They see themselves as "above that type of behavior." What we must accept is "but for the grace of God that would be me."

Many who thought that they were of superior character have found themselves, much to their surprise, in the hog pen of sin wallowing with the best of them. A humble spirit will in most cases keep one from falling. But should the fall happen anyway, one is more likely to fall among friends than in a pen of angry hogs.

Let me leave you with the warning of Oswald Chambers concerning judging others, "If you have been shrewd in finding out the defects in others, remember that will be exactly the measure given to you. Life serves back the coin you pay."

Day 30

WHY IS GOD ALWAYS PICKING ON ME?

Have you ever not wanted to be a "grown up"? There is so much responsibility and accountability. I watch my children playing and laughing and I realize that they really do not have a care in the world. Even when they do something wrong, most of the time they can plead ignorance. Would that not be great to live like that again? Do not misunderstand me, I am happy with my life. But do you ever get tired of being a responsible adult and just want to be a kid again? In many ways we can; but in some ways we cannot.

We cannot become irresponsible like a child when it comes to our relationships with others and with God. We must always do what we know to be the right and mature thing to do. God expects it. He tells me so in His Word, the Bible. Through the scriptures I hear his voice and directions for my life. If I point out the errors of other—He reminds me of mercy and forgiveness. If I point to others—He says that is not you. If I want to rejoice in where I am and what I have achieved—He reminds me of where I came from. Have you ever wanted to ask, "Why is God picking on me?"

Why does He always want me to learn a lesson? Why does He always want me to do what is right when everyone else seems to be doing as they please? I want Him to change others—He wants to change me. I want to be understood—He wants me to understand others. I talk about being justified in my feeling—He talks about forgiveness.

I think I know why He is the way He is. Hebrews 12:5-6 says, "And you have forgotten that word of encouragement that addresses you as sons: 'My son, do not make light of the Lord's discipline, and do not lose heart when he rebukes you, because the Lord disciplines those he loves, and he punishes everyone he accepts as a son.'"

We should not be bothered if it seems that God is always speaking to us about staying on the "straight and narrow". What else would a good father do? We are His children. We should not "make light" of the fact that God disciplines or instructs us nor should we be discouraged because we feel as if we have been corrected.

Because we are His children He will not allow us to get away with doing things that are not right or living in ways that are damaging. We are His children. Therefore He expects more out of us—just as we expect more out of our own children. He is not picking on me. He is dealing with me as His child. He whom He loves He instructs.

Day 31

HOW CAN WE FACE TEMPTATION

As a part of the "Reality TV" genre the Fox Network has produced yet another show of questionable taste and ethics. It is called "Temptation Island." The following is their description from the Fox web site.

"Temptation Island is a short-order unscripted series in which four unmarried couples travel to the Caribbean to test and explore the strength of their relationship.

Once on the island, the couples are introduced to eligible singles and then separated from their partners until the final day of their stay. Over this period, each couple will get the opportunity to answer questions about themselves and one another, and find out if what they think they want is actually what they do want."

The obvious point is to place these people in direct contact with temptation in order to see if they can endure the allure of temptation. In my opinion this is a bad plan from the start. But how many times have we done something similar by not living out our commitment to God?

A survey of *Discipleship Journal* readers who ranked the areas of greatest spiritual challenges in their lives "noted temptations were more potent when they had neglected their time with God (81 percent) and when they were physically tired (57 percent). Resisting temptation was accomplished by prayer (84 percent), avoiding compromising situations (76 percent), Bible study (66 percent), and being accountable to someone (52 percent)."

Note that most people, 81%, people faced their greatest temptation when they had neglected time with God. This should come at no surprise for those of us who know that God is our strength and that God is always FAITHFUL to His people. God's Word assures us of that very thing.

Paul wrote, "No temptation has seized you except what is common to man. And God is faithful; he will not let you be tempted beyond what you can bear. But when you are tempted, he will also provide a way out so that you can stand up under it." I Corinthians 10:13 NIV

Do not miss the most important phrase in this verse, "God is faithful." He is faithful to help us if we will depend on Him. This verse even tells us how He helps us. He has made temptation predictable, He has placed a limit on it, and He has provided a way out.

Once you have done all you know to do to be strong—stand your ground in faith. Stand on the promises of God. Stand on the power of God. Stand on the faithfulness of God. The only solid ground during temptation is the Rock, Christ Jesus!

The victory over temptation may not always be easy but it is possible; the truths of God's Word assure us of this. The victory will be ours when we take what we know of our own weaknesses and what we know of God's power and use the common sense and spiritual senses that God has given us.

God is faithful to help us in times of temptation. He has made it predictable, He has placed a limit on it, and He has provided a way out. It's up to us now. What will we do?

Day 32

WORK ON YOUR SALVATION

Perhaps you have heard someone say, "Everybody has to work out his or her own salvation." After all, that is what the scripture tells us. But how many people have paid attention to what is really being said in that passage? Usually the passage is only used by some to imply that everyone has to decide for themselves what is right or wrong or what direction they will choose for their own life. Given that idea, one might think that the Bible is teaching situational ethics or that it gives us the choice of deciding what is right or wrong. But if we look at that statement "work out your own salvation" in context, we see something very different.

Note the words of Paul, "Therefore, my dear friends, as you have always obeyed—not only in my presence, but now much more in my absence—continue to work out your salvation with fear and trembling, for it is God who works in you to will and to act according to his good purpose." Phil. 2:12-13 NIV

The theme of this passage is found in the statement, "Work out your own salvation with fear and trembling; for it is God who works in you both to will and to do for His good pleasure." The main idea here is not that we decide what's best for ourselves, it is that we should strive to become what God wants us to be. It is not that we should or could earn our salvation, it is that we should live in obedience to God so that people will see that our experience is real.

Sometimes we may feel that God is being demanding in His call for obedience to His Word in all areas. However, he is only challenging us to become more in Christ. And as Paul reveals in our text, our goal should be to see the eternal purposes of God accomplished in our lives. This takes place through our obedience. Paul is telling us that we should, through obedience, work out or work "on" making our salvation all that it is supposed to be.

Too many Christian people decide to ignore the plan of God for their lives when His plan appears to be different from their own. As new Christians we are ready to obey, having neither direction nor a better plan. But as we grow and our lives become blessed, we begin to exert our independence forgetting that it was Christ who has given us the abundant life we enjoy.

When we walk in obedience to Christ we are not only working out our own salvation but we are also working with God who is attempting to accomplish His eternal purposes in our lives. Remember that it is God that is at work within you and He desires to accomplish His will through you.

The question must be asked, "How willing are you and I to respond to God's influence? How committed are you to seeing the eternal purposes of God fulfilled in your life?"

Day 33

WHAT DOES GOD REQUIRE?

On the Statue of Liberty are written the words, "Give me your tired, your poor, Your huddled masses yearning to breathe free, The wretched refuse of your teeming shore. Send these, the homeless, tempest-tost to me, I lift my lamp beside the golden door!" These were the sentiments of a country that, some would say, has long since passed. Yet it was an idea and an invitation that saved many immigrants. Ironically, it seems that the country of immigrants wants to put an end to immigration—except for a certain few. Today I suppose that the plaque on the Statue should read, "Give us your young, your educated, your talented yearning to breathe free..." But some how it does not have the same ring to it. Things have changed and it is not just with the country.

Notice the words of Luke 4:18 and 19. Jesus said, "The Spirit of the Lord is on me, because he has anointed me to preach good news to the poor. He has sent me to proclaim freedom for the prisoners and recovery of sight for the blind, to release the oppressed, to proclaim the year of the Lord's favor." This was the mission of Christ and at one time the mission of the church. But that was a church that many could rightly say is a church long past.

Nevertheless, at one time it was a message that brought hope and salvation to multitudes. When we look at what the organized church has become in many instances in America, it would appear that the church has turned its back on the very people that Jesus cared about. Too many churches have stopped looking for the crowd Jesus sought out. They have to have "the right sort of people" you know. The message from these churches is that there is "good news" for those who want to be rich but not much hope for those who want freedom and relief from oppression.

I realize that some would reduce the church to simply a welfare organization with no spiritual message and others would want to spiritualize everything to the point that human contact is barely necessary. We humans are creatures of extremes. We seem to find the middle ground hard to tolerate.

I realize that there are many good churches and many genuine Christian people. I realize that there are many churches and church-oriented organizations that would and could do more if people would just give to charity a tenth of what they spend on fast food.

But honestly, the problem of unethical religion can only be solved by each of us looking into what God requires of us. The prophet Micah dealt with this same problem many years ago. He wrote, "He has showed you, O man, what is good. And what does the LORD require of you? To act justly and to love mercy and to walk humbly with your God." Micah 6:8 NIV

His message is simple. God's people should set the standard for ethical behavior—both personally and socially. Kindness should define our character and humility before God should be our trademark. It is what God requires of us.

Day 34

GOD'S VALUE SYSTEM

Have you ever been afraid that God would not accept you as you are? Wait before you answer. Really think about it for a moment. Too often we turn away from an encounter with God because we are afraid that He will not respond to us favorably. We know the inner most thoughts of our hearts as well as God does—those thoughts that no one else knows we have.

To add to our discomfort in the presence of God, we also know our failures all too well. Somehow when we try to pray, it all comes before our eyes. We find that it is easier to go on with business as usual rather than to risk being rejected. And yet we hear the voice of God calling us. We know what God wants. He wants us. But why?

He wants us because we were meant to be His. And whether we choose Him or not, He still says that we are valuable. In addition, He offers us something that He sees as extremely valuable—a relationship with Jesus Christ. But we must believe that if we come to Him, He will in no wise turn us away. The scripture reveals the depth of God's willingness to reach out to man in spite of his condition.

Paul said it this way, "You see, at just the right time, when we were still powerless, Christ died for the ungodly. Very rarely will anyone die for a righteous man, though for a good man someone might possibly dare to die. But God demonstrates his own love for us in this: While we were still sinners, Christ died for us." Romans 5:6-8 NIV

These verses contain several undeniable assurances of God's unconditional and accepting love. God's Word says that Jesus deemed us worthy to die for—in spite of the fact that we were not His servants or friends. That is God's value system. He values what some say is without value.

Yet we often have a problem with the truth of our own worth because we have a problem with our value system. The fact that mankind has never been able to merit redemption offends our value system. We see ourselves as the "righteous man" and the "good man" in verse 7 that someone should die for. What we must understand is God's value system. It's not that man is incapable of doing good, it is that the scripture says that man is incapable of being truly good apart from God.

Christ died for us because He loved us, not because we were worthy; it is called grace. Unmerited favor. He loved us without us giving Him cause or reason.

In the earlier verses Paul seems to be emphasizing the apparent incompatibility of human and divine values. Man values those who are right, whole, and lovely because of what they are. God values those who are sinful, powerless, and ungodly because of what they can become.

I wonder how many of us see the value of another human being like God does? Even more, I wonder how many understand the value of a relationship with a God that values us so much?

Day 35

I STILL BELIEVE

Early in my ministry, I served as an assistant pastor to a man who died of cancer. I still remember the last sermon that he preached just a few weeks before his death. His sermon title was "I Believe in Miracles." I suppose that seems something of a contradiction to some, but not to me. This was a man who really did have faith—who really did believe in miracles. Why he did not receive his miracle of healing I do not know.

He was told by one individual, that if he really had faith in God that he would be healed. If that man had only understood the kind of faith that was truly in the life and heart of my pastor he would have walked away in shame for saying such a thing. It is amazing how some armchair theologians who have never faced what others are facing can give such an analysis of another man's faith. The fact is that it does not take much faith to believe in God when everything is everything is turning out the way we want. Sometimes we have to believe with everything going against us—and that is where real faith begins.

My pastor was a good man. He was a godly man. And yes, he was a man of faith who believed in and saw many miraculous things in his life. But the one thing we all wanted and prayed for never happened. But you know what? I am still going to follow his example and continue to believe in the miraculous. Why? Because I still believe in an all powerful and loving God.

In spite of circumstances I still believe that there is a God in heaven that is concerned about our needs. He is not impersonal and aloof. He knows us by name and He cares. If He can call all the stars of heaven by name, how much more does He know your name? (Isaiah 40:26-31) If He clothed the flowers of the field and cares for the little sparrow, how much more does He care for you? (Luke 12:24-29) We are His creation and the "sheep of His pasture." This is why I believe that He cares about us.

I still believe that there is a God in heaven who intervenes in the lives of His people. In other words, I believe that God hears and answers our prayers. No, I do not understand why God does not do some things. Even with years of theological training, at times the ways of God remain a complete mystery. All I do know is this: the here and now is not all there is. But even as mysterious as God seems at times, I have chosen to trust Him. If I do not understand, I will wait. My inability to understand some things will not and cannot destroy His ability to do all things.

Therefore, I still believe that there is a God in heaven that has not lost His ability to do the miraculous. Simply put, I still believe in miracles and healings and divine acts of good done by Him on our behalf. "Why?" some would say. "How can you?" others would ask. I believe because I have experienced that which the Bible talks about. And by His grace I will see it again in my life. And as someone said, "A man with an experience is never at the mercy of a man with an argument." (see Romans 8:33-39)

I know that some may not believe and that is their business. I realize that some may have given up and lost hope. Some may even want to explain away the truth of the scripture. But as for me I still believe.

Day 36

IS YOUR CONSCIOUS YOUR GUIDE?

Have you ever heard someone advise another person on the making of a particular decision, "Let your conscious be your guide"? Is that really good advice? Is that even biblically sound? Let us consider the wisdom of that well used piece of advice.

If we are to put our confidence in our conscience to guide us in all matters then we must consider several important facts. First, although many have a well-defined sense of right and wrong, each person's conscious may differ widely. For instance, some people see nothing wrong with lying or stealing if it will benefit them. Although it is extreme, some people have even committed murder without ever feeling the least twinge of a guilty conscious. Regardless of the extent to which the line of right and wrong is moved by some people, there are enough examples of people following their own individual set of morals to remind us that the human conscious can vary depending on certain factors.

Another problem with using our conscious as our guide is that in general our conscious tends to only be affected after we have done something questionable or wrong. Mostly its influence is felt later when we feel bad about what we did. If our conscious is going to be our guide, should we not be able to count on it every time to keep us from the errors of life before we commit them?

The problems presented by one depending on his or her conscious for guidance are obvious. So what am I suggesting? We must find a higher and more reliable standard or guide on which we can depend.

Some would point to our civic laws as a guide, but the government does not have rules for everything—it only seems that way. Well, what about the Ten Commandments? I certainly think that they should be obeyed. But it is amazing how many people try to reduce them to ten rules or ten suggestions and then work on "bending" or bypassing as many of them as possible.

My solution is to take the whole of scripture as our guide for our actions—in light of the relationship that we are supposed to have with its author. I know some will say, "You can make the Bible say anything you want it to." To which I must respond, "No you cannot, not unless you take it out of context!" And when it comes to scripture regarding human behavior it is often difficult or impossible to misconstrue what is said. Besides, we also have an example to follow not just scripture to read. We can always ask ourselves, "What would Jesus do?"

As long as the human conscious is the final authority on what is proper, the results will vary. But when we take God's standards and His influence as our guide we will see a consistency develop in our behavior that will change our lives for the better.

Day 37

WHAT IT MEANS TO BE COMMITTED

When an airline pilot begins his takeoff down the runway, he continues to accelerate the airplane until he reaches takeoff speed. At that same moment he is approaching the end of the runway. The point of "no return" is reached when he no longer has enough runway to safely bring the aircraft to a stop. At that moment he is "committed" to a takeoff.

When a heart surgeon opens the chest of a heart transplant patient, puts the patient on the heart and lung machine, and takes the diseased heart from the chest of the patient, he is "committed" to the completion of the operation.

When a military general equips his troops for battle, gives them a battle plan, places them in the theater of battle and gives the command to attack, at that point he is "committed" to the battle.

Most importantly, when a person gives his life to Christ by putting his faith and trust in Him and by turning his back on his old life, he is depending on Christ to see him through to the end. At this point we can say that He is "committed."

In each case there is the opportunity to stop all action prior to commitment. In each case there is the danger of disaster if the "commitment" is forsaken. Therefore when we talk about what it means to be "committed," we are making several clear distinctions.

First, we are engaged in something that we have chosen to do. Commitment cannot be forced on anyone. People can be forced against their will to serve, give or participate in an activity—but their commitment is their choice. God will force no one to serve Him. If we live our lives for Jesus Christ, it is because we have chosen to do so. So we must decide if we will be committed or if we will turn back—just do not overlook what is being forfeited. Jesus said, "No one who puts his hand to the plow and looks back is fit for service in the kingdom of God." Luke 9:62 NIV

If we choose to go on from this point, then we have chosen to do something that must be completed. We must now consider the eternal consequences of our decision. If we believe in eternal life, as the Bible speaks of it, then we must remember that what we decide today could determine our eternal destiny. Therefore the call to genuine commitment grows stronger. (Hebrews 3:12-14)

Finally, true commitment means that we have gone past the point of no return. We no longer have a place to which we can return. We have made our choice. We have decided that we must complete our task. And we have passed the point where we could turn back without losing everything. The bridges have been burned. We have sold out to our choice. No matter how many may second-guess us, no matter how our feelings rise and fall, we will press on. This is what it means to be committed.

Day 38

TRUTH OR CONSEQUENCES

If you could do anything that you wanted to do today and there would be absolutely no consequences to your actions, what would you do? What temptation would you face? Think about it for a moment. What you decide will say a great deal about your integrity, character and heart.

First, allow me establish the fact that being tempted, according to the scripture, is not a sin nor does it mean that a person has failed morally. Even the purest of hearts have had improper thoughts or ideas to come to mind. However, it is when we dwell on and act on those things that we go wrong. And that is what we are dealing with. You know yourself. What would you do? What action would you take?

I believe that a great many would live their lives no different that they are right now. For instance, some would not change because they are committed to doing what is right—regardless of who is watching or keeping record. Still others mistakenly think that they are already getting away with what they are doing—so they would not change. But then there are those who would run amuck given the opportunity. They are like the man who consulted a psychiatrist. He complained, "I've been misbehaving, Doc, and my conscience is troubling me." The doctor asked, "And you want something that will strengthen your willpower?" The fellow replied, "Well, no, I was thinking of something that would weaken my conscience."

But still a greater question than, "What would we do?" is "Why do we do what we do?" Do we do the right things because we know that it is expected or because we are right in our hearts? Whatever the motivation of others, the Christian man or woman must consider his/her commitment to Christ.

Proverbs 11:3 tells us that, "The integrity of the upright guides them, but the unfaithful are destroyed by their duplicity." NIV Throughout the scripture the "upright" and "unfaithful" are contrasted—those who are righteous and those who are, literally in this verse, "crooked."

Notice also that the verse says that the "unfaithful" will be destroyed by their crooked ways. Not guided by a sense of integrity, their own actions will bring destruction on them. Yet consider the hope of those committed to the Lord and a life of integrity. The psalmist wrote, "May integrity and uprightness protect me, because my hope is in you." Psalms 25:21NIV

We must choose to trust in the Lord and live a life of integrity and uprightness—not just because of the natural benefits—but because the Lord will honor and bless such a person. The possible consequences or lack of them should not affect out behavior. Only our integrity should determine that. The final analysis is that we can live a life of truth and be blessed or pay the consequences of living an unprincipled life.

Day 39

KNOWING GOD'S WILL

Have you ever struggled with trying to find God's divine will for your life? For the Christian, the will of God must be considered at all times. But at times it is not easy to know God's will. In fact, it is safe to say that anyone who has ever sought God's will concerning a life decision has probably been left feeling a little unsure about what to do—at least for a time. Of course It Is not supposed to be that way, but it is.

In order to get past this problem, let us first look at what we know God's will is NOT. The following applies no matter what the decision may be. We know that it is not God's will for anyone to do anything that is sinful or unethical or anything that would go, in principle, against the teaching of scripture. This eliminates many possible options with which people are faced.

In addition to knowing what God does not want us to do; we can know what He does want. It is God's will that we prosper as our soul prospers (3 John 1:2). It is God's will that we pray, be joyful and thankful (I Th. 5:16-18). It is God's will that we love one another. (I Jn. 3:23) It is God's will that we live holy (I Th. 4:3-5). We could go on and on finding things in the scripture of which the Lord approves. And that is the right place to start. A right relationship with God is the basis for finding any further guidance that we may need. It is the basis for knowing what to ask for as well as the assurance that God will hear us when we pray.

Paul wrote, "This is the confidence we have in approaching God: that if we ask anything according to his will, he hears us. And if we know that he hears us—whatever we ask—we know that we have what we asked of him." I John 5:14-15 NIV If we are committed to living for Christ and are asking for His help in continuing on the right path—we are more than likely praying according to His will.

Furthermore, we have the assurance that if we are willing to follow Him wherever and do whatever He may ask of us, He will make it possible for us to succeed. The writer of Hebrews said, "May the God of peace... that great Shepherd of the sheep, equip you with everything good for doing his will, and may he work in us what is pleasing to him, through Jesus Christ, to whom be glory for ever and ever. Amen." Hebrews 13:21 NIV

I know that most want someone to be able to specifically tell them what decision is right. With God, I cannot guarantee you that you will have a "burning bush" experience. But the assurance is there that if seek to do His will; He will guide us. As someone wrote,

> "Before us is a future all unknown, a path untrod;
> Beside us a friend well loved and known-
> That friend is God."

Day 40

GOD'S DISCIPLINE

Why is it that we tend to think that everything that happens to us of a negative or difficult nature is always to our detriment? Even we have missed the mark, sinned, or erred in our lives we seem to feel that there should be no negative results to our actions. After all, we repented and missed a blessing. Is that not enough?

I suppose that our mindset has something to do with the society in which we live. Many Americans have come to believe that everything in their lives is supposed to be good and, if it is not, then it is either the fault of someone else or God has failed them. After all, if no one else is working to please them at least God is supposed to be.

The fact is that our relationship with our heavenly father is much like that of a natural relationship between a good parent and child. Just as a good parent sets guidelines and metes out discipline and correction for the good of the child, so our Heavenly Father does the same—but with absolute perfection.

Hebrews 12:5-11 asks us to consider the importance of God's discipline. "And you have forgotten that word of encouragement that addresses you as sons: 'My son, do not make light of the Lord's discipline, and do not lose heart when he rebukes you, because the Lord disciplines those he loves...'" NIV

Being disciplined spiritually should actually encourage us. I can say this because God's discipline is not abusive, but rather instructive. Therefore the Lord's discipline should never be rejected. Instead we should rejoice that we are accepted as His children.

The writer of Hebrews goes on to say in verses 7 and 8, "Endure hardship as discipline; God is treating you as sons. For what son is not disciplined by his father? If you are not disciplined (and everyone undergoes discipline), then you are illegitimate children and not true sons." NIV

Again, we see the evidence of God's love in the manner in which He deals with us. It is good to remember that the heir will always receive the necessary instruction.

Finally in verses 9-11 he says, "Moreover, we have all had human fathers who disciplined us and we respected them for it. How much more should we submit to the Father of our spirits and live! Our fathers disciplined us for a little while as they thought best; but God disciplines us for our good, that we may share in his holiness. No discipline seems pleasant at the time, but painful. Later on, however, it produces a harvest of righteousness and peace for those who have been trained by it." NIV

Regardless of how other may have led us, we can always count on our Heavenly Father to lead us to a deeper spiritual life. Even with the best intentions earthly parents make mistakes. However, God's discipline is "good" and always produces a blessing.

The desire to "feel good" spiritually is natural. But when we attempt to achieve a good feeling while ignoring the prodding of the Holy Spirit, we only do damage to our spiritual life. Instead of focusing only on our feelings, we should be focusing on the results of God's work in our lives.

Day 41

SHOULD GOD ANSWER ALL PRAYERS?

I heard someone pose the question, "What if we lived in a world where all prayers were answered, what kind of a world would it be?" I had never thought of that possibility before. But let us consider it for just a moment. At first it might appear that it would be a great world in which to live. But upon further examination of that idea we might find that our supposed "great world" has some flaws.

Let us begin with a look at God. What kind of god would we have if He were a god who answered ALL prayers? Stop right there for a moment. You and I both know that there have been some selfish, foolish and even evil prayers uttered by humanity. What kind of a god would answer those types of prayers? It could be argued that God would be reduced to a cosmic errand boy at best, and humanity's servant at worse. He certainly would no longer be sovereign. He really would not even be just or fair. He would only be what we made Him—our slave.

But wait. What if He only answered good or "right" prayers, would it be a bad world then? No? Well, who is going to determine which prayers are good or right? Who knows what is best in all situations? Who can know the future? Who can know the heart? Sure God does. But remember, God doing what He has thought best is what started people questioning and criticizing Him in the first place. If we let Him decide, then we may not get what we ask for. Then what? Will we accuse Him also? Will we be angry with Him?

Most would probably respond, "How could we accuse Him, He is the only One who knows what is right and wrong in every situation? He is the only One who knows the future. If we are going to believe that prayer works we must leave it all in God's hands." So, on second thought, having a god that would answer all prayers does not sound so good.

At this point let me say that I do not have any idea why God does not answer some prayers. I just have to recognize that He knows all and I must leave it all in His hands. In all my times of confusion and wondering I must rely on what I do know.

Note what David wrote, "For the LORD is righteous, he loves justice; upright men will see his face." Psalms 11:7 NIV We need to be reminded that not only is God righteous, both upright in character and in actions, He also loves to do what is right.

So when I pray I realize that I am depending on a God who knows all things, loves all people, who is perfect in character and loves to do what is right. This is why I can trust Him to answer my prayers as He sees fit.

Day 42

GOD HAS PLANS FOR YOU

How many times have we fallen short of receiving God's best in our lives because we were not convinced of His good intentions or else His ability to do what was needed? Or was it because we did not feel deserving of God's help or blessing? We sometimes tell ourselves that we were not meant to have certain things or to accomplish certain goals, and we do so without ever consulting God on the matter. Yes we pray, but do we listen?

In his book, *My Utmost for His Highest,* Oswald Chambers asks the question, "Have we ever let God tell us any of His joys, or are we telling God our secrets so continually that we leave no room for Him to talk to us?" What are His joys? Are they not His plans for our lives?

In Jeremiah 29:11 God reveals His heart and mind to humanity. As He had before and would so many times again, He said, "'I know the plans I have for you,' declares the LORD, 'plans to prosper you and not to harm you, plans to give you hope and a future.'" NIV

Do not run past the implications of the first part of that passage. The wonderful truth revealed here is that the God of all creation, the Eternal One, is thinking about us. We are flattered when we receive a card in the mail from someone who has thought of us. And yet right here, God is thinking about us and we run right past it.

"But God knows everything. Of course He is conscious of us." Some would say. Still others ignore the fact that God is thinking about them and just want to know what judgment or blessing awaits them. While God does warn us of the consequences of sin and sends blessings to those who love Him, there is more going on here than that.

What I want you to see is that God is not merely aware of us, He is not out to get us and He is certainly not just a source of blessings. I want you to listen to what He is saying, "'I know the plans I have for you,' declares the LORD, 'plans to prosper you and not to harm you, plans to give you hope and a future.'" Allow me to paraphrase. "You know what? I have been thinking about you and what you can become and I want to do something for you. I want you to prosper. I want to give something to look forward to in life. I want you to have a good life."

Note that the tone of His words is that of a benevolent father who is offering the child that he loves a once in a lifetime opportunity. I realize that everyone cannot relate to the "good parent" metaphor, but if we could have a perfect parent or father—it would be God. And you know what? We can.

He is waiting on us to believe in His pure intentions. We do not have to deserve it. Besides who could? We just have to accept it. God has been thinking about you for a long time. Why not listen to what He has planned for you?

Day 43

ARE WE NO LONGER IN AWE OF GOD

Do we really believe in the greatness of God? It would seem, at times, in our gospel saturated society that we have either lost or abandoned our understanding of God's greatness. In our desire to make God acceptable and understandable to everyone I think that we have, in a sense, degraded Him and done a great injustice to His character and person.

In the arrogance of humanity we see the idea promoted that, through the study of theology, we can come to a place that there is nothing about God that we cannot understand. However, I do not believe this to be true. If anything, the study of theology has revealed to us a God that is beyond our understanding.

Note what God said about Himself, "For my thoughts are not your thoughts, neither are your ways my ways," declares the LORD. "As the heavens are higher than the earth, so are my ways higher than your ways and my thoughts than your thoughts." Isa.55:8-9 NIV

One of the first truths that we must remember about God is that He is not like us. As humans we try to make Him as much like us as possible, but it will never work. He is altogether righteous and perfect, which in itself, places Him beyond our understanding. But why should this frustrate us; do we have to know or be able to explain everything? Why can we not just stand in awe of His person?

Note the words of the psalmist as he marvels at the glory and power of the creator. He writes, "Praise the LORD, O my soul. O LORD my God, you are very great; you are clothed with splendor and majesty. He wraps himself in light as with a garment; he stretches out the heavens like a tent and lays the beams of his upper chambers on their waters. He makes the clouds his chariot and rides on the wings of the wind." Psalm 104:1-3 NIV With a God like that, how could we understand everything about Him? We know no one like Him. We must be content with the fact that He chooses to reveal Himself to us in various ways and in varying degrees, but never fully because our minds cannot comprehend the divine.

Sometimes I think the reason that we have such a problem with not being able to understand God, is that we wonder if He is really at work for our good. After all, if He were working for our good why would we not understand His actions as such? We will leave the mysteries of the universe to God if He will only answer a few basic questions. Standing in awe of God is fine; just let me know the answers to a few of the concerns on my mind. That sounds reasonable, does it not?

Reasonable or not, we are simply left to stand in wonder and awe of a God who is, at times, mysterious and incomprehensible. Many of our questions will be answered when we step into eternity. But for now we must rest in the fact that the God of eternity loves and cares for us. That in itself is wondrous.

Day 44

FAITHFULNESS PRECEDES SUCCESS

Success is not a word that you will find very often in the scriptures. And when it is used, it is never used as we in America have often come to define it. As Americans we tend to interpret scripture from the perspective of a modern day prosperous society, with our goals and values inserted. We have even "Americanized" the gospel to the point that it has almost been reduced entirely from the gospel of Christ to a success strategy that will lead us to ultimate happiness and great wealth.

Every year, many graduate from high schools and colleges around the country. And in keeping with the American dream, they are generally hoping to go out into the world and be successful, happy and wealthy. This is as natural as it is common. And none of these things are necessarily wrong. Some will pursue their dream by adding more education, some by going straight into the workforce, and some by seeking out new life experiences. Each one, no doubt, wanting to be successful at something. But will seeking success above all else really make them happy?

When it comes purely to the pursuit of success, I really do not think that even if we dress it up and send it to church that it will fit into God's plan for our lives. We could even go so far as to say that "success" is not a Biblical concept that the scripture promotes. Am I saying that God does not want us to be successful? No. I am just saying that it is not a life-goal that is ever promoted by the Word of God.

Then what does the Bible promote? It promotes faithfulness. Faithfulness always comes before any godly successes in life. Perhaps faithfulness is the goal God wants us to strive for because "success" is entirely subjective. What one considers to be success, another may care nothing for at all. Perhaps it is because success in this world rarely seems to satisfy or maybe it is because the pursuit of success usually makes one more focused on one's self.

What we do know is that the characteristic of faithfulness in a person's life will often lead them to personal satisfaction. It will affect others in a positive way and bless them because faithfulness is relationship oriented. Whether we are faithful to our spouse, our family, ourselves, our integrity or to our God, we are building relationships and character and forging a life that will often find itself caught up in many successes.

It goes against the grain of our society to focus on our character rather than our careers or to consider God's will rather than our wants, but that is exactly what God wants us to do—go against the grain. Paul said, "Do not conform any longer to the pattern of this world, but be transformed by the renewing of your mind. Then you will be able to test and approve what God's will is—his good, pleasing and perfect will." Romans 12:2 NIV

For those seeking to find happiness and true success in life, Paul's advice was good then and it is still good now.

Day 45

WHAT HAS LOVE GOT TO DO WITH IT?

I preached a message a couple of weeks ago in which I questioned the actions and attitude of the prophet Jonah. In particular, I questioned whether or not Jonah was unloving and maybe even held bigoted views toward the Ninevites. I went on to point out that Jonah certainly did not deserve to be viewed as the hero of the story. My comments raised more than one eyebrow. So let me be clear, I do not have a bad attitude toward Jonah.

But it is my desire to point out something that many Christians refuse to see about a man who has been used as a role model in some cases. Therefore, let us look at the facts. His bringing the message of God to them saved One hundred twenty thousand people. This was good. But should we overlook the fact that he only brought the message because he believed that God would kill him if he did not? Should we overlook the fact that he was a hate-filled man, just because he saw results? Understand, he did not have a bad attitude—he wanted 120,000 people to die. It certainly was not his compassion or concern for the Ninevites that touched their hearts.

One of the biggest problems with the church in America is that we justify our "attitudes" and even our hatred of certain people by pointing to our grand church building, our bank accounts, what we do for missions, our handouts to the poor and we go home at night and rock ourselves to sleep at night believing that everything is fine with our hearts because we did a few good works. Yet our attitudes and our hearts remain unchanged and unmoved. The truth is that if we hate people, we are no more conformed to the image of Christ than was Jonah.

What about what Paul said in I Corinthians 13:1-3? "If I speak in the tongues of men and of angels, but have not love, I am only a resounding gong or a clanging cymbal. If I have the gift of prophecy and can fathom all mysteries and all knowledge, and if I have a faith that can move mountains, but have not love, I am nothing. If I give all I possess to the poor and surrender my body to the flames, but have not love, I gain nothing." NIV

Without love we accomplish nothing of any eternal value. We are nothing no matter what the church reports say. Such behavior cannot be tolerated or whitewashed—much less accepted—no matter what the results. As the book of Jonah closes out, God is trying to get something across to Jonah. It was like God was saying, "You still don't get it, do you? The value of all humanity, the lesson, my love, my character—you have missed the whole point of it all."

If you have not read the book of Jonah—read it. You might just see something about Jonah, and even yourself, that you have never seen before. And by the way, the hero of the story is God.

Day 46

COINCIDENCE OR PROVIDENCE

A friend of mine recently went on a missions trip to Uganda. He was visiting a group of churches that he had been to many times before. They were glad to see him and welcomed him as usual. Although it was not unusual for him to take gifts with him when he went, when he opened a suitcase filled with basic medical supplies, they began to cry. Obviously they were thankful, but there was something more behind their gratitude.

A few weeks before he was to return to Uganda, he had mentioned the various needs and progress of the churches. One particular situation that he mentioned caught my attention. I remembered him saying that everyday items that we take for granted, like Tylenol, were kept under lock and key—if the people could secure any. I did not think much about it until one day when I felt impressed that I should have my church collect basic over-the-counter medical supplies and give them to my friend to take with him on his upcoming trip. Another church joined with us and we were able to send all types of medical supplies in a large quantity.

We sent the supplies and thought nothing more about it until my friend returned and he told the story about how the people had cried when they saw the supplies. That in itself was not unusual; people often cry when happy or thankful. But the something more was this. About the same week that we felt that we should send medical supplies to Uganda, the church in Uganda was praying and felt God was impressing them to start a hospital for the local people who had no one to care for them.

Now you must understand that a hospital in rural Uganda is much different than a hospital here in America. It would be a difficult task for the people even though their hospital would consist of not much more than a structure with a roof and some beds. Nevertheless, they found a small vacant building and a few beds, but as they told God, they had no medicine and no way to get any. Yet they would not give up; they would do what they could.

Then their old friend from America came to see them and what do you think that he had for them? It was the medicine, of course. And that is why they began to cry when they saw the large suitcase of medical supplies. God had sent the much-needed medicine from the other side of the world because they were willing to do what He had led them to do.

I know that some would say that it was all just a coincidence. Out of all the trips that he and others had made, no one had ever felt that they should take medical supplies. And never before had the church ever felt that they should start a hospital. Coincidence? I think it was providence. This should serve to remind us that when we feel as if we should do something good for someone, we do not always have to stop and ask why or how. We can just do it. Who knows? We might have a part in someone's miracle.

Day 47

WHY DO GOOD THINGS HAPPEN TO BAD PEOPLE?

It is an age-old resentment. Someone who is viewed as a bad person has something good happen or prosper greatly in life. Instantly, those who have done what was right all their lives, but who have had less prosperity, question why. Why, God, would you allow a person like that to have all those good things happen?

Listen to the psalmist in Psalm 73:1-5. "Surely God is good to Israel, to those who are pure in heart. But as for me, my feet had almost slipped; I had nearly lost my foothold. For I envied the arrogant when I saw the prosperity of the wicked. They have no struggles; their bodies are healthy and strong. They are free from the burdens common to man; they are not plagued by human ills." NIV

The psalmist had looked at life and said, "I know God is good to His people, but I struggle with why evil people prosper so much in spite of their evil ways." Sound familiar? The psalmist had lost his perspective. I can tell this because he was beginning to believe things that simply were not true. He was believing things such as all wicked people prosper; they have no struggles; they are all healthy and strong; and they do not have any burdens or problems. Of course this was not true—but it seemed that way to him at the time.

Read on through the psalm and you will hear more familiar complaints. But as you do, you will also receive the same revelation, as the psalmist did. Note just this one excerpt: "When I tried to understand all this, (how the wicked seemed to prosper) it was oppressive to me till I entered the sanctuary of God; then I understood their final destiny." Psalm 73:16-17 NIV

Allow me to point out an obvious fact from this passage. If a person is truly evil and is prospering that person does not have it as good as you think because that person must still face God. The fact is that no one who fails to repent will get away with doing anything evil—not even the most religious person.

Now, let me ask you. Should God limit or prevent people from having anything good in their lives just because they are perceived by us to be bad? Who knows, God may just be at work in their lives. Who knows, they might not be as bad as we think in some cases. Paul, in Romans 2:4, tells us that the goodness or kindness of God leads men to repentance. We have already seen that God will punish evil. But God will try every way possible to avoid it, just like a loving parent would. He has no pleasure in judgment.

Allow me to conclude with a couple of questions rather than answers. If we feel like the psalmist or have had the same thoughts, why is it that we have our eyes on others? Why have we allowed ourselves to become envious of others? And even if someone is evil, what makes some people want to see others suffer?

Day 48

NO REASON TO ENVY WRONGDOERS

I would like us to consider further the questions of why and how it seems that some people who ignore God and do evil seem to prosper or at least seemingly face no consequences for their actions and why it seems that people who do good suffer adversity. In doing so we need to consider some facts that perhaps have been overlooked.

First, God has not been deceived by anyone. Not only is He the only one who can judge the heart of another, He is also qualified to do so. Paul tells us, "Do not be deceived: God cannot be mocked. A man reaps what he sows. The one who sows to please his sinful nature, from that nature will reap destruction; the one who sows to please the Spirit, from the Spirit will reap eternal life." Galatians 6:7-8 NIV Simply put, no one fools God.

There is an immutable law of God at work in this world in spite of what some may think. The way we live our lives matters. It will matter to us one day if it does not already and it certainly matters to God right now. In the Old Testament He phrased it this way, "I am setting before you today a blessing and a curse..." Dt.11: 26-28 NIV We have a choice in life in what we receive out of life. We can have a blessed life.

A second fact to consider comes in two parts. First is that when we see evil go unpunished we could in reality be seeing the judgment of God at work. According to the scripture the absence of punishment is evidence of the judgment of God in a person's life. There are people who God no longer warns. Consider Romans 1:28, "Furthermore, since they did not think it worthwhile to retain the knowledge of God, he gave them over to a depraved mind, to do what ought not to be done."

When the day comes that a man no longer regrets his evil actions and seems to no longer suffer any consequences for wrong doing, it is a day to fear—not a day to celebrate.

Now we come to the second part of this truth. When we see people pay for doing evil it is actually the mercy of God. I know that may sound odd to some. We always tend to feel that if God does not forgive, forget and make it all better that He does not love us. In reality, the fact that He allows us to suffer when we do wrong could be one of the greatest signs of His love. Why? "Because the Lord disciplines those he loves, and he punishes everyone he accepts as a son." Hebrews 12:6 NIV

There is much more to consider, but for now let those who are doing right NOT be envious of those doing wrong—for any reason. Neither allow yourself to feel that God does not care about you because all your problems do not vanish. And finally, to those who are doing what is morally or spiritually wrong and feel no negative effect—you will reap what you sow.

Day 49

THE DIVINITY OF DIRT

I realize that I am probably not the first to have this thought, but as I was watching one of those educational channels I was reminded of something that I have never heard explained by scientists. They can explain anything you know.

It all goes back to what I learned in high school and college science courses. My confusion centers on the atom. Although the atom is so small that it can only be seen by high-powered microscopes, it is still considered the basic building block of all matter. Everything is made up of atoms. Every molecule of air, water or earth is made up of atoms. This I understand. What I want to know is where the atom came from. Forget trying to explain how the universe was formed and the origin of man; tell me where the basic building block of ALL things came from.

As a means of keeping it simple, put aside the atom for a moment; let us use the origin of dirt as the focus of our question. It is a common substance found anywhere in the world. Technically, it is found in one form or another, everywhere in the universe. What is its origin?

There are really only three possibilities or explanations. First is the idea that dirt has always been. It has existed eternally. It has always existed and will always exist. Can you imagine dirt existing without beginning or end? It sounds supernatural to me. But what about the "Big Bang Theory"? That only attempts to explain the formation of the universe, not where "matter"—the rocks, dirt and gases came from. Well, that's a dead end—unless you believe dirt has always been and will always be.

There is another possible explanation. Dirt came into existence on its own. It created itself out of nothing. Wow, dirt with creative powers! Not only that, it existed before itself. Huh? That's right. It had to exist prior to its creation if it were going to create itself. It could not create itself unless it was there to do so. It sounds to me like dirt could be, dare I say it, God like.

There is one other explanation that I do not know if I should even mention in this educated and "enlightened" world in which we live. But here goes: someone of a divine nature and existence created dirt. There I said it. What an outdated notion that is! But what am I to do? I cannot believe that dirt has always existed and will always exist entirely on its own. Nor can I believe that dirt, existing before itself, created itself out of nothing.

You will just have to overlook this unenlightened fellow. I am going to continue to believe in a divine being, God, who existed before all things, created all things and will exist after all things. It just makes more sense to me than believing in, what is actually, the divinity of dirt. Now, if you want to believe in the divinity of dirt or that dirt has supernatural powers—be my guest. I have just one request. Send me your name and address. I have some oceanfront property in Nebraska I need to sell.

Day 50

SMALL DOUBTS DESTROY BIG PRAYERS

Do you believe that you must beg God for an answer to your prayer? Do you believe that you must earn His action on your behalf? If you said yes to either then you have misunderstood the nature of prayer.

There are two necessary actions for us to take if we are to see our prayers answered. These actions are found in James 1:6-8. James writes concerning the man who prays, "But when he asks, he must believe and not doubt..." NIV

From this passage we see that it is necessary for us to ask for God's help. Do not waste time hoping that God will do something or that "the good Lord will meet your need" when you have never asked Him to do so. People like that are usually the ones who get angry at God for not doing something for people as "good" as they are.

If you have a need, simply ask God to meet that need. Prayer is the basis for making all of our requests known to God. If we doubt the value of bringing our petitions to God then we are stopped before we ever start. If you ask something of God, then expect generosity from Him. It is the nature of God to be generous to those in need.

Next, it is necessary for us to believe that God will help us. In general, it has appeared to me in my encounters with people in hospitals and funeral homes and other difficult and tragic places that people want to hear me express only three basic truths in the words that I say. First of all, people want to hear the truth that "God loves them"; not that He has a love for them but that He loves them personally. Second, they want to hear that God cares about them— again not in a vague way—but He cares about what they are presently going through. And third, they want to know that God is going to help them. He is going to somehow intervene in their situation and make a difference.

In times of need, the human heart often reaches out to God and desires desperately to believe. It is not a desire that God takes lightly. He wants us to believe and He wants to answer even if our prayers and faith are not perfect. Ideally, we are not to entertain any doubts whatsoever. But every prayer is not the ideal prayer. Take for example the father in Mark 9:24-27. The man brings his afflicted son to Jesus, asks Jesus to heal his son and is then questioned by Jesus if he believes. He states, "I do believe; help me overcome my unbelief!" NIV He knew that he had to overcome his unbelief in order to receive. Jesus worked with him where he was—a struggling soul—and healed his son.

If you and I doubt and do not attempt to overcome our doubt, there is no reason to believe that you and I will receive anything from God. In short, a person who doubts does not have a made up mind. Our minds must be set on asking and receiving—even if we know we are weak in that area. Those small doubts are what threaten to destroy our prayers.

Day 51

DANGEROUS SUPERSTITIONS

I have noticed something over the last year or so that has me concerned. Although it is nothing new, throughout the history of Christianity there have always been periods of time when people within the church have mixed superstitious ideas with faith in Christ. It would seem that either faith in the Word of God and prayer are not enough for some or else they insist on inserting certain "extra ideas" about the supernatural realm into what the scripture has already told us.

In particular are two instances that point to this fact. First there is the electronic chain letter that usually tells the recipient to "read this prayer out loud three times and forward it to seven people in the next five minutes and God will bless you" or answer your prayer or whatever. Do people really think that this is the way prayer works? If so allow me to offer these two passages, first from 1 Timothy 2:5-6 which reads, "For there is one God and one mediator between God and men, the man Christ Jesus, who gave himself as a ransom for all men..." NIV

A "mediator" is a go between. Jesus is the one who makes it possible for us to speak to God about our needs. We receive from God because of Jesus not because of sending or receiving a letter or an e-mail. Hebrews 4:15-16 tells us, "For we do not have a high priest who is unable to sympathize with our weaknesses, but we have one who has been tempted in every way, just as we are—yet was without sin. Let us then approach the throne of grace with confidence, so that we may receive mercy and find grace to help us in our time of need." NIV

The second idea is closely related to the first and that is that some think that the scripture can be used as an incantation. Case in point, the way some have used the prayer of Jabez. A good book was written on the subject but evidently some missed the point. Jabez had a relationship with God and that is why the prayer worked. However, some have the idea that if one just repeats it or "prays" it over and over that he or she will be blessed—even if there is no relationship. Still others think that it is the magic prayer that brings wealth when prayed.

Maybe they are like the people Jesus dealt with in John 6:26. These were people with no interest in encountering God, but rather in having their belly filled. "Jesus answered, 'I tell you the truth, you are looking for me, not because you saw miraculous signs but because you ate the loaves and had your fill.'" NIV In another place Jesus had this to say to those who were preoccupied with material things, "But seek first his kingdom and his righteousness, and all these things will be given to you as well." Mt 6:33 NIV

Let me be clear. For a Christian, it is through Jesus Christ that our assurance and peace is secured—not through chain letters or e-mails or through repeating a "magic" prayer over and over. It is through knowing God and having a personal relationship with Him that we find all that we need.

Day 52

JESUS CAN JUGGLE

The other night as my wife was trying to get my five-year-old to sleep my daughter was telling her that she had been having bad dreams at night. My wife told her that she should ask Jesus to help her have good dreams. "Can He do that," she asked? "Of course He can," her mother replied. "He can do anything." "Really," my daughter asked in questioning amazement, "Can He juggle?" "Yes," came the response, "He can even juggle!"

My wife and I had a good laugh over that one. But obviously being able to juggle is impressive to a five-year-old. The understanding of a child is often complicated and sometimes amusing. Right now their questions and responses make us laugh as well as make us think. But as parents we know that one day their understanding will mature and their thinking will become clear about most things in life.

I wonder if God is waiting on the same thing to take place in our lives. No doubt most of us have been reassured about God's ability to help us in our time of need and have heard about how powerful that He is. Yet, as if in the same questioning amazement of a five-year-old, we respond, "Yes, but can He or will He do this?"

What is it that we find impressive about God? What can He do that will convince us that He will take care of us or help us in our time of need? It is not that God does not want to be put to the test. (Mal. 3:10) But why must we always need to take a wait-and-see attitude about depending on God? Has He not ever helped us? "But you do not understand! If I could just see God do something then I would and could believe." Would we?

Take note of the story of Israel's deliverance from bondage and their subsequent attitude. "He divided the sea and led them through; he made the water stand firm like a wall. He guided them with the cloud by day and with light from the fire all night. He split the rocks in the desert and gave them water as abundant as the seas; he brought streams out of a rocky crag and made water flow down like rivers. But they continued to sin against him, rebelling in the desert against the Most High. They willfully put God to the test by demanding the food they craved. They spoke against God, saying, "Can God spread a table in the desert? When he struck the rock, water gushed out, and streams flowed abundantly. But can he also give us food? Can he supply meat for his people?" When the LORD heard them, he was very angry; his fire broke out against Jacob, and his wrath rose against Israel, for they did not believe in God or trust in his deliverance." Psalms 78:13-22 NIV

All of these supernatural feats performed by God in the past should be enough to convince us, at the very least, that He is surely able to "juggle" the difficulties and problems we face in our lives— and make them work out in our favor to boot! The only question that remains to be settled is when our faith in Him will reach its maturity.

Day 53

GROWING OLDER

I noticed something the other day when I got out of my recliner. My body sounded like a bowl of Rice Crispies. Snap. Crackle. Pop. I am not very old but at times my body feels it. Which made me think of what life would be like for me and for this body of mine when I really am a senior citizen.

Many say that life has never been better for seniors in our society. There are more advantages for senior adults than ever before. If you have read Tom Brokaw's book *The Greatest Generation,* it is possible to see that maybe there is even a new respect for those who are in our oldest generation. And it seems that even Wall Street is after the lucrative senior dollar.

Yet everything does not seem to be getting easier for those who are aging. In fact, some seniors are more unhappy than ever before. I realize that some may have made their life what it is and there is not much that anyone can do to change it—much less make them happy. But I think some have legitimate complaints.

This is not reality for everyone, but it is easy to see how some feel that it is their reality. Put yourself in the place of a senior adult in their "declining years and declining health." Everybody seems to think that you are on your way out. Consequently, your opinion may not be considered. People now speak to you as if you do not have good sense. You were a part of the rat race and mainstream society and now others just want you off the road and in a home.

With this in mind, to senior adults I say take heart. Not everyone feels the way some appear to. You are valuable and have much to offer. Get involved in life. The abundant life that Jesus promised to those who trust in Him does not have an expiration date on it. Become involved with young people as much as possible. It will keep you young and, besides, you have a great deal in common— middle-aged people do not think that either of you have good sense.

Remember the words of Paul, "Teach the older men to be temperate, worthy of respect, self-controlled, and sound in faith, in love and in endurance. Likewise, teach the older women to be reverent in the way they live, not to be slanderers or addicted to much wine, but to teach what is good." Titus 2:2-3 NIV

To the younger generation, especially in the church, wake up! You really do not know everything. How would you like to be told to give your offering but keep your opinions to yourself? Do you want to know what Jesus would do (WWJD)? He would show respect.

Remember what Paul wrote to the young minister Timothy, "Do not rebuke an older man harshly, but exhort him as if he were your father. Treat younger men as brothers, older women as mothers, and younger women as sisters, with absolute purity." I Timothy 5:1-2 NIV

In short, I think God's Word teaches us that age should not matter where our behavior is concerned. And it certainly teaches that our value is not diminished by our age.

Day 54

WHY WE RECEIVE FROM GOD

I heard something the other day on a television program that concerned me. The person speaking was promoting the idea of "sowing a financial seed" in order for one to receive a miracle. Now I believe in giving financially to the church or to God's work in various forms. I believe in tithing from one's income to support the church. I believe in miracles. However, when one starts connecting the giving of money with receiving healing for his or her children or spouse—I get concerned.

The reason for my concern is that it is likely that people will begin to feel as if they have to buy the blessings of God. Maybe they will believe that their financial gift to God somehow influences God's decision to help them. Even worse is the possibility that some will feel that God owes them a miracle because they "paid Him off." The connecting of miracles of healing with gifts of money somehow seems to tarnish the character of God and call into question His holy character. The very idea that we need to, or can, persuade God to help us by giving something is a complete misunderstanding of who He is.

What the Bible does teach about money is that when we honor God with the "firstfruits" of our money that He will provide a way of being even more blessed in the future. (ex: Malachi 3:10 & Lk.6:38) There are also many other passages that speak of God providing for His people if they will put Him first in their finances.

What the Bible teaches about having the other needs of our lives met is also clear. First, if one knows Christ as Savior and Lord then he or she can come to Him and ask what he or she will because of their relationship—not because of his or her bank account. Jesus taught, "Ask and it will be given to you; seek and you will find; knock and the door will be opened to you. For everyone who asks receives; he who seeks finds; and to him who knocks, the door will be opened." "Which of you, if his son asks for bread, will give him a stone? Or if he asks for a fish, will give him a snake? If you, then, though you are evil, know how to give good gifts to your children, how much more will your Father in heaven give good gifts to those who ask him!" Matt. 7:7-11 NIV

There can be a fine line between teaching that many blessings come out of obedience to Christ as opposed to the idea that what we do persuades God to help us. The fine line is blurred when we emphasize our desire to receive over our relationship with Christ or when we think that God can or needs to be bought. What gives us our balance is in knowing the true nature and character of God in a personal relationship. Therefore, we should set our minds on keeping our relationship with Christ as it should be and not on trying to determine what we must do to merit God's intervention in our lives.

Day 55

THE PROBLEM WITH GRACE

Nothing seems to cause some Christian people more problems than the grace of God. Some want to preach an intolerant God, which demands holiness to the point of complete personal perfection. Still others want to preach a God so tolerant of sin that no one is ultimately held accountable for his or her actions.

The problem is that when decide that a person has been forgiven enough and, therefore, deserves no more forgiveness, we are drawing lines that only God can draw. We have misunderstood the nature of the grace of God. God forgives those who are repentant, not those who achieve a certain perceived level of personal perfection and not those who are better Christians or even those who seem to have an easier time obeying God.

I realize that it is very easy at this point to preach a God that ignores sin or winks at our transgression. I am not doing that because it is not the truth. Neither am I promoting the idea that God becomes intolerant of us because of our failures and our sins. The truth is somewhere in the middle where God judges each according to his or her heart, actions and behavior. It is simply our willingness to repent and ask God for forgiveness that makes the difference between those who find the favor of God and those who do not. Some are willing to repent, and do so genuinely, and some do not. God knows the difference.

Our challenge is not to declare boundaries but to present a balanced God. Too many times we present a God that is like a human being—intolerant. In addition, we sometimes present a God who ignores sin like we often do. Sadly, humanity not only makes excuses for itself without limit but also condemns itself without mercy. Thankfully, God is not like humanity. God is perfect, righteous and holy. Sometimes that goes against everything that we feel is right. But the person in error is always you and me—not God.

Our bias, our upbringing and our philosophy of life will influence so many things about us. But God is not influenced by society, by parents or by peers. Therefore the question that should be asked most often is, "Why does it seem that some want to condemn people and see them cut off?" Do they feel that they are members of the spiritually elite or do they really have a zeal for God? Do they feel as if God is hard and unbending toward them and thus toward everybody? As well we could ask, "Why do some want to excuse sin and overlook error?" Could it be that they have too many sins that they want to whitewash, overlook and ignore and, therefore, they are willing to do that in the lives of others. Even the very questions we ask cause us to draw conclusions that we are unqualified to make.

The duty of judging or forgiving is not ours but God's alone. Our calling is to proclaim the truth of God's Word and of His character. Every person will give an account of his or her life. Still one question remains, "What damage will we do in the process, or what good will we do, of leading people to God?"

Day 56

THE HEALER OF BROKEN HEARTS

Has your heart ever been broken? Was it due to a tragedy, a relationship, unkind words or disappointment? Broken hearts are often the result of many different causes, but they are broken nonetheless. One of the most memorable words on this subject comes from the movie classic, *The Wizard of Oz.* Remember when the Wizard says to the Tin Man, "Hearts will never be practical until they are made unbreakable"? Practical or not, we have them and they do break.

The good news is that there is a Healer of broken hearts who can work wonders with the fragile pieces. The psalmist wrote of the Healer, "He heals the brokenhearted and binds up their wounds." Ps. 147:3 NIV David wrote, "The LORD is close to the brokenhearted and saves those who are crushed in spirit." Ps. 34:18 NIV Of course, Jesus is the healer of whom I speak. And I just want to remind the broken hearted of some very important truths born out in scripture.

First, He is near. "The LORD is close to the brokenhearted," not metaphorically or symbolically, He is there. I experienced His presence first hand at the graveside of my brother on the day we buried him. I remember sitting there feeling overcome with grief when the words of the scripture came to me. Although I did not hear a voice, it was as if God was standing there saying to me, "I will not leave you without comfort, I will come to you," (John 14:18) and I felt as if I could make it. Something happened in me, because He was there.

Next, He wants you to know that His purpose is to heal. That is why He is there. Isaiah foretold that Jesus would be sent to "bind up the broken hearted." Isaiah 61:1 I cannot promise that you will have all your questions answered—I wish you could--but sometimes healing is more important than knowing. How He can take the broken pieces and put them all back together again I do not know. But, as for me, I have learned that He can do it when no one else can.

Thirdly, He is able to save those who have been crushed. Remember the words of David, "The LORD is close to the brokenhearted and saves those who are crushed in spirit." A broken heart can leave a "crushed spirit," but Jesus will never leave a heart halfway restored. I do not know how that I can explain this other than to say He will put life back into your heart.

Contrary to the hopes and even beliefs of some, good and godly people do not always escape heartache. Broken hearts are as common among those who believe in Jesus Christ and do what is right as there are among those who do not. But for those who will believe, there is a Healer of broken hearts that is always near, ready to help and can put the pieces of our hearts back together again.

Day 57

WHEN GOD FELT HUMAN

Have you ever felt forsaken by God? If not, perhaps you have felt that at times there was a distance or a separation between God and yourself that left you feeling alone when you were experiencing difficult times. I have felt that way before. Of course, I do not believe that God will forsake us. But it is certainly an emotional sensation that many have experienced and that can be very real. It is all part of the human experience that not even being a Christian can prevent.

To illustrate, allow me to direct our attention to Jesus and His earthly life. Jesus was God incarnate, which means that He was both completely God and completely man—something beyond our comprehension but true. However, what we do understand is that He lived a life much like ours. He slept or rested when He was tired, He ate when He was hungry, He laughed, cried, became angry, made friends and made enemies—just like any other human. But what we overlook is that He felt the burden of being human even in His interaction with God the Father.

Listen to His words prior to the crucifixion as He prayed in the garden, "My Father, if it is possible, may this cup be taken from me. Yet not as I will, but as you will." Matt. 26:39 NIV This simple statement tells me that the burden of being in a human body was weighing heavy. Now listen to His words as He hung on the cross. "About the ninth hour Jesus cried out in a loud voice... 'My God, my God, why have you forsaken me?'" Matt. 27:46 NIV He was not merely quoting the words of David in Psalm 22:1, "My God, my God, why have you forsaken me? Why are you so far from saving me, so far from the words of my groaning?" NIV

He was feeling what David and you and me and other human beings have felt throughout history. He was feeling human and it was not the first time. For thirty-three years He had felt human in every way that we do. The writer of Hebrews said it this way, "For we do not have a high priest who is unable to sympathize with our weaknesses, but we have one who has been tempted in every way, just as we are—yet was without sin." 4:15

The beauty and power of this truth becomes evident in the next verse. "Let us then approach the throne of grace with confidence, so that we may receive mercy and find grace to help us in our time of need." 4:16 NIV When you and I wonder, "Why God?" or, "Where are you God?" or even, "Lord, must I go through this?" there is One seated beside God the Father who knows those questions and knows those feelings and is ready to offer sufficient grace and mercy to help us in our time of need.

Day 58

SURVIVING IN THE RACE OF LIFE

Nascar fans are a devoted lot. They seem to be fascinated with the race and all that is involved. Their hope is that their favorite driver will cross the finish line first and their biggest fear is that he will hit the wall. If the driver hits the wall it could mean the end of the race for him or, at worse, the end of life.

I have heard people speak of "hitting the wall" before but usually they are not talking stock car racing. I have heard that expression used as another way of saying that one has "come to the end of his rope." In other words, it is used to describe the feeling of being emotionally exhausted or devastated. When one "hits the wall" emotionally, the person has in essence been hit hard by life.

Using the imagery of a race, allow me to make several observations about the race in which we are all involved—the race of life. I have noticed, in car races as well as in life, that there is usually an obvious reason that one hits the wall. Sometimes it is due to a bad decision by the individual, but sometimes it is due to another's decision. At times it is due to trying too hard or getting careless. Whatever the reason, a person can find himself in trouble quickly when life goes out of control.

Secondly, not everyone who hits the wall survives. What a tragedy it is to see a life destroyed by a mistake or a wrong turn. In a car race it can happen in an instant. But in life it usually happens more slowly. That is why we must be observant of those around us. When we see that someone has "hit the wall" emotionally, we must not take it lightly. Without encouragement and help and prayer they may not make it. Simply put, suicide or a breakdown is often the result of "hitting the wall" emotionally.

But the good news is that it is possible to "hit the wall" and walk away. I have seen many horrible accidents on the track where the car was destroyed yet the driver walked away to race another day. For those who have "hit the wall" or may do so in the future, the Bible offers hope in Christ.

Paul wrote, "For God, who said, 'Let light shine out of darkness,' made his light shine in our hearts to give us the light of the knowledge of the glory of God in the face of Christ. We are hard pressed on every side, but not crushed; perplexed, but not in despair; persecuted, but not abandoned; struck down, but not destroyed." 2 Cor. 4:6-9 NIV

No one is exempt from the hard knocks of life, as Paul clearly points out, but we can survive with God's help. We are not crushed, in despair, abandoned or destroyed. God will see us through.

Always remember the encouraging words of Paul, "Being confident of this, that he who began a good work in you will carry it on to completion until the day of Christ Jesus." Phil. 1:6 NIV

Day 59

WILL WE PASS THE TEST

Recently the United States has been and is being put to a great test. Terror, destruction and a state of war has reached our nation. No longer will we watch the world news stories about terrorism and the destruction of crazed suicide bombers in other countries and say to ourselves, "I am glad that that does not happen over here." Now, it happens here and as many have repeatedly said, "America will be forever changed."

Our president tells us that we are up to the test. Our military leaders tell us that we are up to the test. But how do we as a country pass such a test? If we blow the enemy off the face of the earth, will we have passed the test? Obviously something has to be done militarily and I am confident that it will be done well. But what about you and me and every other citizen, not involved in retribution, security and politics—what will we do? How will we fare?

America, as a whole must come together to face this first major crisis of the new millennium without being greatly scarred or changed in some adverse manner. The way in which we conduct our everyday lives, as well as the moral and social decisions that we make, will no doubt have a profound effect on our nation in the coming months. So, what must we do?

We must not lose faith in one another as human beings. I do not mean just American people but all people. We live in a global society whether we like it or not. People from a number of other nations were killed in the World Trade Center along with Americans. Other nations are genuinely standing with us at this time of grief and destruction that not only we, but that the world, has also suffered. It is easy to hate and distrust everyone unlike ourselves but it is not right. Everyone different is not evil. We must take the intelligent and wise high ground even when we retaliate. If we become a warlike and vengeful people filled with hatred for all foreigners and other nations—we are no better than the terrorist that attacked us.

In addition, we must not give up our faith in God. Whether some like it or not, it is often been faith in God that has brought us together and put us back on track throughout history. Religion is not the problem. The cowards that attacked us and others like them only hide behind religion as they have throughout history. They were extremist. Their real agenda is not pleasing God but destroying others not like themselves. America, it is time to pray, but is also time to live a life pleasing to God.

In short, there is more to passing this test than taking revenge and making our enemy pay. How we come together and what our ultimate goals are will determine if we will pass the test. And as I see the images of survivors, rescuers, volunteers and compassionate countrymen, I, too, have faith that we will pass this test.

Day 60

ATTITUDE COUNTS

I have two daughters. They are as different as daylight and dark. One is like me and the other is like my wife. The other day I asked my five-year-old if she had had a good day. She replied, in a voice that made me know she thought my question was silly, "I always have a good day!" Are people like that annoying or what? She is like her mother. They are the kind of people who awake and say, "Good morning Lord!" Whereas, my two-year-old and I awake and say, "Good lord, it's morning!" Needless to say, we have to work harder on our attitude than do they.

But you know, I do not think that my youngest and I are alone in our struggle. In fact, it is probably due to the fact that everyone experiences times when his or her attitude is not the best that the Bible addresses this very situation. The scripture helps us out not only by telling us that we all need to work on our attitudes but also by telling us what the Christian's attitude should be.

First, Paul wrote in Ephesians 4:22-24 that our attitude should be different than it was before our conversion. "You were taught, with regard to your former way of life, to put off your old self, which is being corrupted by its deceitful desires; to be made new in the attitude of your minds; and to put on the new self, created to be like God in true righteousness and holiness." NIV

He speaks of having a servant's attitude in Philippians 2:3-5. "Do nothing out of selfish ambition or vain conceit, but in humility consider others better than yourselves. Each of you should look not only to your own interests, but also to the interests of others. Your attitude should be the same as that of Christ Jesus..." NIV

He speaks of having a positive attitude in Philippians 4:8. "Finally, brothers, whatever is true, whatever is noble, whatever is right, whatever is pure, whatever is lovely, whatever is admirable--if anything is excellent or praiseworthy—think about such things." NIV

He even speaks of having a triumphant attitude in Romans 8: 35-39. "Who shall separate us from the love of Christ? Shall trouble or hardship or persecution or famine or nakedness or danger or sword? ...No, in all these things we are more than conquerors through him who loved us. For I am convinced that neither death nor life, neither angels nor demons, neither the present nor the future, nor any powers, neither height nor depth, nor anything else in all creation, will be able to separate us from the love of God that is in Christ Jesus our Lord." NIV

Obviously our attitude is important to God. But His reason is not that He simply wants us conform to His will and way of thinking, but that our everyday lives be enriched and made more profitable. At this point, it is simply up to us to begin the process of change that will result in a good attitude. So, here we go everybody. "Good morning, Lord!"

Day 61

THE LIGHTS IN THE DARKNESS

One of the most beautiful sights that I have ever seen is that of a star-filled night sky. There is something glorious about, not only the sight, but also the immensity of it all. Yet, as someone once observed, the stars are only visible during the darkness. They are the lights in the darkness. An obvious truth, but a truth that can nevertheless stand as a reminder of how we often do not see all the beauty and value of life until dark times.

It happens everyday. Somewhere, someone is coming to the realization of how blessed that he is because of some tragedy or heartbreak that he has observed in another's life. Maybe he has just been spared of bad news, got an undeserved break or blessing or for some other reason just realized how fortunate that he was. Whatever the cause, he is now awake to the blessings of his life.

Oddly enough, the blessing were there all the time—just like the stars. We know the stars are present during the day as well as during the night, but because of the brightness of the sun they only become visible once the sun has ceased to shine. Likewise, too often the blessings of our lives are overlooked because of the easiness and blessedness of our life. To put it bluntly, most Americans do not realize how good we have it in this land of freedom that we call home. Blessings and good things are all around us and yet we pass them by without even noticing. We have our reasons for our blindness, but they are in most cases only pitiful excuses.

Not too long ago I was leaving my parent's house at night. They live in a rural area, far from the glare of streetlights. When I looked up, I was amazed at the brightness and number of stars that I saw. I told my wife that I could not see the stars from our home in the city and that I had forgotten how beautiful they were. After we returned home, I was unloading the van and busy getting everything inside, when my wife, who was standing in the drive looking up, said to me, "You can see the stars from here. You just have not been looking." And you know what? She was right. I could see them clearly. I just had not been looking.

That brings me to my point. First, we need to open our eyes and behold all of our blessings. Once we see the blessings in our lives we should then recognize them for what they are—evidence of God's unmerited goodness in our lives. Therefore, every time we see or recognize a blessing in our lives we should give glory and praise to God.

If we think about it, those same stars in the night sky are speaking to us and reminding of God's wonderful goodness in our lives. King David said it this way, "The heavens declare the glory of God; the skies proclaim the work of his hands. Day after day they pour forth speech; night after night they display knowledge. There is no speech or language where their voice is not heard." Psalms 19:1-3 NIV

What a beautiful way of remembering to be thankful for God's goodness. Each time we see the stars, the lights in the darkness, they should serve to remind us to praise God even in adversity.

Day 62

WORK ON YOUR SALVATION

Perhaps you have heard someone say, "Everybody has to work out his or her own salvation." After all, that is what the scripture tells us. But how many people have paid attention to what is really being said in that passage? Usually the passage is only used by some to imply that everyone has to decide for themselves what is right or wrong or what direction they will choose for their own life. Given that idea, one might think that the Bible is teaching situational ethics or that it gives us the choice of deciding what is right or wrong. But if we look at that statement "work out your own salvation" in context, we see something very different.

Note the words of Paul, "Therefore, my dear friends, as you have always obeyed—not only in my presence, but now much more in my absence—continue to work out your salvation with fear and trembling, for it is God who works in you to will and to act according to his good purpose." Phil. 2:12-13 NIV

The theme of this passage is found in the statement, "Work out your own salvation with fear and trembling; for it is God who works in you both to will and to do for His good pleasure." The main idea here is not that we decide what's best for ourselves, it is that we should strive to become what God wants us to be. It is not that we should or could earn our salvation, it is that we should live in obedience to God so that people will see that our experience is real.

Sometimes we may feel that God is being demanding in His call for obedience to His Word in all areas. However, he is only challenging us to become more in Christ. And as Paul reveals in our text, our goal should be to see the eternal purposes of God accomplished in our lives. This takes place through our obedience. Paul is telling us that we should, through obedience, work out or work "on" making our salvation all that it is supposed to be.

Too many Christian people decide to ignore the plan of God for their lives when His plan appears to be different from their own. As new Christians we are ready to obey, having neither direction nor a better plan. But as we grow and our lives become blessed, we begin to exert our independence forgetting that it was Christ who has given us the abundant life we enjoy.

When we walk in obedience to Christ we are not only working out our own salvation but we are also working with God who is attempting to accomplish His eternal purposes in our lives. Remember that it is God that is at work within you and He desires to accomplish His will through you.

The question must be asked, "How willing are you and I to respond to God's influence? How committed are you to seeing the eternal purposes of God fulfilled in your life?"

Day 63

WHY SHOULD I CARE

Have you ever been doing your best and trying to retain all of your weary character only to get the feeling that others had long since given up on both? There you are doing your best, to be your best, and what have you got to show for it? If you have ever felt that way, then you also know that the next thing to enter your mind is going to be the question, "Why should I care?" It is at that moment that you will make the decision between being a person of character and just another broken soul on the heap of discouragement, or worse yet—a person without character.

The fact is that there are many reasons to care when it would seem that few others do. First of all, you should care because it matters—at least for you. The decisions that we make are the ones with which we will have to live. We, alone, lie down with our thoughts and conscience every night. With our words we may try to reason or justify a "devil-may-care" attitude. But when we are alone with ourselves, we will find it hard to accept such an attitude. Why? What we think of ourselves matters—that is why.

Next, there is nothing of value gained by giving up. I said nothing of value. Sure, we could come up with some perceived benefits. We can always look around and see others who seem to have "stopped caring" who also appear to be faring better than we are. In fact, their list of reasons why they have decided to take the path of least resistance is filled to capacity. However, it will be difficult to find anything of true value on that list. What people who have stopped caring have really given up is a part of themselves. They have evidently forgotten that there is great satisfaction in knowing that we are still intact after we have passed up the temptation to sell off part of ourselves.

For one who is striving to serve Jesus Christ, the idea of not caring or selling out our principles cannot even be entertained. The Christian life demands that we care. No, there is not a commandment that says, "Thou shalt care!" But the life, mission and goal of true Christianity calls us to care deeply about our walk with Christ in every area of commitment.

Paul expressed his sense of commitment when he wrote, "I eagerly expect and hope that I will in no way be ashamed, but will have sufficient courage so that now as always Christ will be exalted in my body, whether by life or by death. For to me, to live is Christ and to die is gain." Philippians 1:20-21 NIV

Paul knew that there was nothing of value lost in being committed when others were not, yet what was to be gained was of eternal value. The value was eternal because of the life received through the commitment. In the case of a Christian, caring makes an eternal difference. Caring is commitment—in this life and in the next.

"For none of us lives to himself alone and none of us dies to himself alone. If we live, we live to the Lord; and if we die, we die to the Lord. So, whether we live or die, we belong to the Lord." Romans 14:7-8 NIV

Day 64

UNDERSTANDING THE VALUE OF YOUR FAITH

We value what we most understand and love. I have always known that, but I was made keenly aware of it one night when my wife and I went to the symphony. We are not really "symphony people" but our neighbors were nice enough to give us their two tickets when they were unable to go. My wife is a musician, she plays the trumpet, and I, well, I play the radio. To make matters worse, culturally speaking, I am at best, in my wife's words, a reformed hayseed.

The night of the symphony we dressed up and I prepared myself for an evening of culture. There we sat enjoying the music, my wife pointing out the "subtle nuances" to me (the things I was missing); it was beautiful. But then at the end, when the final note was played, a man in front of me leapt to his feet with others and began applauding wildly. My first reaction was to look and see if they had seen something that I had not. Then it hit me. Evidently, I did not hear what he, my wife and others had heard. I heard the music fine, but I did not hear it with the appreciation of one who understands and plays music.

As a Christian, I often find my self in a somewhat similar situation. I am sometimes in the situation of trying to communicate or defend my faith to those who do not believe or are in the process of trying to make sense of Biblical truths. As a rule, although they may respect my beliefs, they do not truly appreciate my faith in Christ. They can see the moral value, the psychological benefits and even the social good will, but they are missing it as much as I was Beethoven's genius.

Paul explains the problem this way, "The man without the Spirit does not accept the things that come from the Spirit of God, for they are foolishness to him, and he cannot understand them, because they are spiritually discerned." 1 Corinthians 2:14 NIV It is no wonder that without the Holy Spirit, the Bible is just a collection of stories to them.

So allow me to encourage those who hold faith in Christ dear to their hearts and want others to know and experience it as well. Your faith makes sense to you because of the Holy Spirit who lives in your heart. You faith will never truly makes sense to others in the same way as long as the Holy Spirit is absent from their hearts. God's love for them is the same. It is only that the "realness" of His love is missing.

So maintain your faith, though misunderstood and sometimes ridiculed. Your faith is real and the Biblical message is true. As Paul reminds us, "You show that you are a letter from Christ, the result of our ministry, written not with ink but with the Spirit of the living God, not on tablets of stone but on tablets of human hearts. Such confidence as this is ours through Christ before God... He has made us competent as ministers of a new covenant—not of the letter but of the Spirit; for the letter kills, but the Spirit gives life." 2 Corinthians 3:2-6 NIV   May the Spirit add His life to the heart of those who seek God.

Day 65

GOING FOR THE GOLD

One of my parishioners asked me one time if I ran for exercise. They had seen someone running down the road one day that they thought looked a good bit like me. I'll tell you what I told them. If you ever see me running anywhere—do not ask questions—just run, too, because something very big is after me!

I got my fill of running in high school. My freshman year I ran track for a man who was a fanatic about running, to say the least. "Boys," he would say, "if you want to be champions you have got to be willing to do at least three things—sweat, bleed and throw up." Wow! I was motivated. Please excuse the sarcasm, but let's get real, who looks forward to that?

I remember a good bit of sweating (a total of nine miles a day was mandatory). I even remember running enough that I wanted to throw up, but I never bled. Maybe that is why I was never an Olympic champion and never won a gold medal. But then again, maybe coach played too many years of football before they issued helmets to players. Whatever the case, I ran that year and then went back to baseball which was somewhat less demanding.

In a way, I think that most of us want to choose the easier path of life and the more attainable goals over the road of hardship, sacrifice, discipline and even pain. The problem is that all goals cannot be reached on the path of least resistance. There is often a great struggle involved in reaching the greatest victories and blessings.

In spite of what some may think, Christians struggle toward a present goal—that of finding God's will for their lives. There is also the need to accomplish His will, as well as an eternal goal of entering into life's final reward. It is not uncommon for Christians to struggle with their faith—not because God is making it tough on us, but because human beings do not always seem to be able to see past their own feelings.

Job was a man who struggled with his own set of difficulties while trying to follow God. Notice his words as he searches to make sense of all that God is doing. He says, "But if I go to the east, he is not there; if I go to the west, I do not find him. When he is at work in the north, I do not see him; when he turns to the south, I catch no glimpse of him. But he knows the way that I take; when he has tested me, I will come forth as gold." Job 23:8-10 NIV

Job's words sound familiar when he says in essence, "I cannot see God" and "I cannot figure out what He is doing." But read on. He expresses his faith and our hopes when he tells us what he does know. Allow me to paraphrase, "God knows where I am and when the test is over I will have been purified like gold!"

A pastor friend of mine told me that he had used this scripture to encourage a woman in his congregation who was going through difficult times. As she started to leave she pause at the door and asked him, "Pastor, do we really have to go for the gold?" If we want to be champions, we do.

Day 66

THE STRUGGLE OF THE SOUL WITHIN

The affects of Cerebral Palsy appear devastating in many ways. With CP the messages from the brain to the muscles are disrupted. This causes disturbances in the motor functions of the human body. Simple movements of the body that most take for granted are difficult to control or even achieve by a person with CP. Simply put, their brain may tell their body to move a certain way, but the body will not and cannot obey.

However physically debilitating this may be, it does not affect one's ability to think, to feel, to love, to hurt. There are many brilliant and loving people who have CP, but who are also often thought of as being "retarded" by those who are ignorant or unaware of this condition. The contrast between the true person and the outward bodily function is so great that we might even say that there is another person contained in the unruly body of the person with Cerebral Palsy.

Spiritually speaking, we all have our imperfections that hinder us from fulfilling the will of our heart and mind. Sometimes, people who want to live for Christ have difficulty getting their outward life to submit to the their inward will. The problem is two-fold. First, some apparently think that all their imperfections have been removed or that they should be overlooked because of what has taken place in their heart. Either way, they are hindered in their spiritual walk because the outward person seems, at times, unruly and will betray their heart or mind. This can be devastating because of the way others perceive them.

The second aspect of the problem involves the attitude of judgmental individuals who write people off because of any perceived failure in their Christian experience. These are usually members of what I call, "The Holier Than Thou Club." These people fail to see why and how others can fail.

What we all must understand is that every person is different. Every situation is different. Ultimately, each must learn to allow Christ to help them in the way and to the extent that He wants to help them. God's power is not limited—but our understanding of His power is—and until we all have the same understanding we cannot all be forced into the same mold.

Jesus Christ starts with the heart and does some of His work instantly and some of His work gradually. I believe strongly in the transforming power of Jesus Christ—but not everything happens instantly for everybody. I know people who gave up drunkenness instantly, but still struggle with their temper. Sin and spiritual failure are spiritual ailments that affect our outward life at times.

So, what do we do? We continue to trust in Christ and work on our relationship with Him regardless of whether we measure up to everyone's standards. God's standard is all that matters. It is in the power of Christ to keep you and perfect you. Note the praise of Jude for Christ. "To him who is able to keep you from falling and to present you before his glorious presence without fault and with great joy—to the only God our Savior be glory, majesty, power and authority, through Jesus Christ our Lord, before all ages, now and forevermore!" Amen. Jude 1:24-25 NIV

Day 67

THE DIFFERENCE BETWEEN SUPERSTITION AND FAITH

Several years ago I heard a radio preacher offer a toll free number for his listeners to call if they wanted to know how to obtain "good luck" according to the scriptures. It would have been hilarious if it were not for the fact that it blends superstition and Christianity and that some people were financially and intellectually taken. Let me assure you, in case you did not know, the secret to "good luck" or any other kind of "luck" is not found in the scriptures.

What we find promoted in the scriptures is faith. I realize that some may be saying, "What's the difference?" Well, this is the difference. Superstition is defined as, "An irrational belief that an object, an action, or a circumstance not logically related to a course of events influences its outcome." Whereas faith is defined as, "Confident belief in the truth, value, or trustworthiness of a person, an idea, or a thing; belief that does not rest on logical proof or material evidence." (American Heritage Dictionary)

Superstition is first of all illogical and fear based. It is a belief where there is no proof that a given event and the outcome are related. For example, there is the belief that black cats bring bad luck. Imagine someone who believes that their traffic accident is related to having a black cat run across the road in front of them prior to the accident. They would associate the black cat with the accident and assume the bad luck caused by the cat was the cause. Now if you drive as much as I do, then you know that black cats are not the reason for accidents—it is more likely crazy or inattentive drivers. In fact, the reason the cat is running is probably because it saw them coming!

Now let us look at faith. Faith is confident in the truth and is not connected to "material evidence." Some of the features of faith are mentioned in Hebrews 11:1, which says, "Now faith is being sure of what we hope for and certain of what we do not see." Faith is something on which a person can base his life. In fact, it is faith that gives us the ability to build our lives on unseen realities made real to us by the truth of God's Word.

I could point to recent studies published in various magazines concerning the very real benefits of prayer and faith. But I do not want to imply that we can or should base our faith purely on empirical evidence. I want us to understand that the truth of God's Word and the character of His person are enough! Faith is the foundation for all that is "hoped for" and it is what assures us "of what we do not see."

We know that faith is real and that it works, because we know that God has stood the test in the past. In fact, He wants us to put Him to the test today—to truly place our trust and confidence in Him to provide as He has said in His Word. Therefore, faith is only irrational and superstition-like if one does not know the character and trustworthiness of God. But if one truly knows God, then he also knows that only the cats need to be afraid.

Day 68

THE INCREDIBLE POWER OF TRYING

When I began college I had a psychology teacher who said something that I will never forget. Some in the class had been complaining about the difficulty of the material. So, she responded by asking if there was anyone in the class who was brain damaged. Surprised by her question, everyone answered with a "no." I think some were lying. But nevertheless, she asked one more question. "Has anyone ever been told by a doctor that you were mentally impaired to the point that you are incapable of learning?" Once again everyone responded that they had not. "Then" she stated, "You can learn anything. It may take you longer than some but you can learn if you will try."

This was a powerful revelation to me because I was a good ten years older than everyone, starting a second career, and feeling a little lost my new pursuit. But from that day I made up my mind that I could learn anything if I would try. I determined that it could not hurt to try and so I would. Since then I have enjoyed many success and accomplishments that I formerly never dreamed possible.

This is not to say that I have achieved any form of greatness. I am not famous, I am not wealthy and I am certainly do not feel that I have impressed everyone. But my point is that I am happy. I see my goals as attainable, not impossible. I see my life as blessed, not doomed. This happened, in part, because of my decision to try.

Recently, my younger sister met one of my professional associates—which one I do not know. Upon hearing that I was her brother he said, in what she said was a patronizing tone, "Yes, I know Mark. He has potential." Frankly, his words irritated me. I recited to myself everything positive that had happened in my life and accomplishment in my career and thought—the nerve! Maybe it was just pride on my part, but it seems with some people that no matter what one accomplishes it is never "good enough" and that is annoying.

But the more I thought on it, the more I realized that he was right. I doubt that he meant to compliment or encourage me but you know what, I do have potential! I remember what Paul said, "I can do everything through him who gives me strength." Phil. 4:13 NIV And he also said in Romans 8:37 that "We are more than conquerors through him who loved us." NIV

For me the incredible power of trying is more than a philosophy of life—it is a reality of life. Sure, a positive mental attitude is important for me, but so is knowing Jesus Christ. The power of trying, and for trying, is found in the support of Jesus Christ and the Holy Spirit. It is more than attitude; it is assurance. It is about more than what I can do, it is about what He can do with me and through me.

You know what? I have potential and so do you. Make up your mind that you will try. Call on the Lord for help and watch what great things will begin to happen in your life.

Day 69

ONLY THE STRONG SURVIVE

I suppose that you have heard the old saying or maybe even the song that says, "Only the strong survive." It goes along with the "survival of the fittest" philosophy that teaches that those who are strong prevail and those who are weak perish. That is the way it is on the nature channel—out in the wild of the animal kingdom. However, even though things may get wild in our kingdoms at times, human beings face a much different world than do animals.

However, when considering the "survival of the strong" philosophy that some have, the question comes to mind, "What if you and I fall into the weak category?" Age, sickness, emotional stress, can all take their toll on human beings and weaken even the best of us. So, if we should find ourselves feeling weak, should we just give up? If we cannot muster the strength to stay on top, what else can we do?

We trust in the Lord, much the same way as did the Apostle Paul. Paul had his own "weakness" of sorts that hindered him in his life. He even prayed that the Lord would remove it. Yet, listen to the answer he received, "But he said to me, 'My grace is sufficient for you, for my power is made perfect in weakness.' Therefore I will boast all the more gladly about my weaknesses, so that Christ's power may rest on me. That is why, for Christ's sake, I delight in weaknesses, in insults, in hardships, in persecutions, in difficulties. For when I am weak, then I am strong." 2 Corinthians 12:9-10 NIV

When our weakness is too great, we can always find refuge and help in the Lord. We can be strong even when we are weak because it is not our strength upon which we are depending. We are

90

depending on the Lord. David expressed his confidence this way when he said in Psalm 7, "O LORD my God, I take refuge in you; save and deliver me from all who pursue me, or they will tear me like a lion and rip me to pieces with no one to rescue me." (v. 1-2) David realized that he lived in a world when the strong dominated the weak and he was feeling weak. Yet he did not lose hope because of the Lord.

You and I may not always be the "strongest." We may even feel at times to be among the "weak" of this world. The truth is that we are not beasts of the animal kingdom doomed to a certain end, nor are we expendable in the eyes of God. We will survive this life— and the one beyond--because of Jesus Christ. His promise to us is that even when we are weak we are strong.

Others can live by that "dog eat dog" mentality if they want to, but without a refuge, they need to consider that one day they will be on the menu. Why not put all your hopes for survival in the One whose strength never fails?

Day 70

WE NEED TO TALK

Have you ever had someone want to speak with you about something, but would never come out with what they had to say? It can be frustrating for the one who is willing to talk, but who has to endure a seemingly endless amount of idle chitchat. Perhaps you could help them, answer their question or resolve a problem, but you will never know because they will not come to the point and tell you what is on their mind.

I wonder if God gets frustrated with us in the same way? After all, He knows what we need before we ask Him and yet we tend to be timid about really pouring our heart out to Him. He awaits dialogue with us, yet He only gets chitchat. Who knows what answers and blessings await us? Too many of us have been left wondering all because we did not just come out with it!

When it comes to human-to-human relationships I can understand that sometimes we do not know how the other person will respond, hence we are unsure of our words. We even fear communication with certain people. We may wonder, "Will he or she understand?" That uncomfortable feeling and the unanswered questions about the other's response combine to become a hindrance to our ability to communicate.

Well, let me assure you that those worries need not apply with God—even if you feel that you are a terrible sinner. That is usually why most are afraid to pray. Listen to the heart of God, even when speaking to a sinful nation, "Come now, let us reason together," says the LORD. "Though your sins are like scarlet, they shall be as white as snow; though they are red as crimson, they shall be like wool. Isaiah 1:18 NIV God has no desire to punish or destroy people, especially those who are willing to communicate with Him.

Furthermore if you and I are trying to live a Christian life, God wants us to feel a freedom and even a sense of being welcomed into His presence through the act of prayer. The writer of Hebrews tells us, "For we do not have a high priest who is unable to sympathize with our weaknesses, but we have one who has been tempted in every way, just as we are—yet was without sin. Let us then approach the throne of grace with confidence, so that we may receive mercy and find grace to help us in our time of need." Hebrews 4:15-16 NIV

Do not miss the essence of this truth. Because we have a Savior that knows and understands how we feel and what it is to live in this world, He has chosen to help us communicate with God the Father. He makes it possible for us to find mercy and grace and help when we are in need. He knows how badly we need to come together with God and talk—to reason together—to bear our souls to God.

Leave the chitchat and the uncomfortable feelings to human relationships. The answers, the help, and the blessings await us if we will get to the point in our conversation with God.

Day 71

PREPARE YOURSELF TO WIN

Every time a new year rolls around people start making resolutions—as if that is the only time of year we can start over. These "New Year" resolutions usually deal with our health or appearance. From past experience I know that in the first few weeks of the new year I will encounter a good number of people who are on diets. Also, as I have experienced before, there will be crowds flocking to the gym or the health spas until at least the end of February. The regulars will be red-faced because they are annoyed at having to wait for a machine and the new- comers will be red-faced because they cannot inhale enough air and are on the verge of passing out.

Getting back in shape physically is tough, as many will find out in the coming weeks. Perhaps that is why, come March, there will be no more lines for the treadmill or the Stair Master. Things hurt that we forgot we had, muscles pull, and the progress is slower, hotter and less glamorous than we had hoped. We find we do not look good in spandex—for that matter no one does except the models in the magazine—and that is not us. And to top it all off, we are pushed for time with our busy schedule. The ones that will last are the ones who take their goal seriously and simply refuse to quit.

The problems are similar for those who want to improve their spiritual lives. Some who have dropped out of church will come back. Some who are in church will seek to revive their experience. Both decisions are great, even better than the resolutions about the physical needs. Like those seeking to improve their health or appearance, the ones who truly reap the spiritual benefits of pursuing a life of faith will be those who take their goal seriously and refuse to quit.

The Apostle Paul uses the image of an athlete in training for competition to convey powerful truths about our need to take seriously our spiritual walk with Christ. He writes, "Do you not know that in a race all the runners run, but only one gets the prize? Run in such a way as to get the prize. Everyone who competes in the games goes into strict training. They do it to get a crown that will not last; but we do it to get a crown that will last forever. Therefore I do not run like a man running aimlessly; I do not fight like a man beating the air. No, I beat my body and make it my slave so that after I have preached to others, I myself will not be disqualified for the prize." I Corinthians 9:24-27 NIV

Let me encourage you to take Paul's advice in your spiritual pursuit. Focus on the purpose of your pursuit, not on the perceived results. Results will vary from person to person, but God will honor faithfulness. Remember that what you are working for is of eternal value. Do not be haphazard or careless in what you commit yourself to—this decision is the big one. And finally, like Paul, do not allow your passions or natural desires to keep you from your goal. Like an athlete who takes on a strict regimen of training, prepare yourself to win, and by God's grace you will.

Day 72

GOD WELCOMES YOU AS YOU ARE

When I was about twelve years old, I was asked to be in my cousin's wedding. It was being held at a large Catholic church in the city where my cousin lived. Being from a rural area and usually only attending a very small church (and that only on Easter and Christmas), I was unfamiliar with religious matters to say the least.

That is why upon arriving at the church for rehearsal, and needing a place to hang my coat, I thought it only logical to use one of the closets that lined the back wall of the Catholic Church. But as it turns out, those are not closets. Next, when I sat in the pews I found out that those comfortable "foot rests" are not foot rests, but altar benches on which people are supposed to kneel. Let me tell you what else I learned, in case you do not know these things, when the man comes down the center aisle swinging the smoking incense, first of all, he knows that it is smoking and second—no it is not on fire—it is "smoldering." But if it were on fire, there is enough water in the "birdbath" up front to put out the fire. Which, you guessed it, is not a birdbath after all.

Few people are as unlearned in the area of church and religion as I was at twelve; still after years as a pastor I have found that many find religion a bit confusing. Some feel lost in our services. Some feel that not knowing how to participate in the services will hinder them from being heard by God. Still others become so preoccupied with the thought of not doing something wrong that they miss out on an encounter with God.

There is nothing wrong with ceremony or having a prescribed way of doing things. Every church, regardless of denomination, has its rituals and preferred form. In fact, church services would be confusing for everyone if there were no order. However, when the order and the ceremony and the form become the main attraction, we have missed it. People need to come to church to encounter God, but too often we complicate the process.

Fortunately for those who want to know God, Jesus has made it simple to understand. First, He wants us to know that He freely accepts anyone who comes to Him in faith. No form needed—just faith. In fact, Jesus promised that, "Whoever comes to me I will never drive away." John 6:37 NIV There is no need to worry about being rejected by God.

Secondly, all we need to bring with us is a humble heart. The psalmist wrote, "The sacrifices of God are a broken spirit; a broken and contrite heart, O God, you will not despise." Psalm 51:17 NIV And thirdly, He wants us to know that He can completely transform our lives when we put our trust in Him. The writer of Hebrews assures us, "He is able to save completely those who come to God through him, because he always lives to intercede for them." Hebrews 7:25

I can assure you will all confidence that our Heavenly Father looks for us to come to Him. He listens to hear us pour out our hearts to Him. And He waits for us to give Him the opportunity to work in our lives. Let me encourage you to seek to know God today.

Day 73

IS GOD'S LOVE ENOUGH?

God's love is simply the most pure and most wonderful love that humanity could ever know. It motivates a holy God to forgive and be merciful to unholy, and many times, unkind human beings. However, some have so overemphasized the love of God as to give the impression, and add to the belief, that God is so loving and benevolent toward humanity that all will enter heaven one day no matter how they have lived, what they have believed, or whom they have followed.

I would even go so far as to say that in our American culture many are frightened to herald any other type of God for fear of severe criticism and rejection. Even now as I write this, I wonder if some will misunderstand what I am about to say. Nevertheless, I must say that true Christianity is not based solely on the love of God. As Christians we cannot even say that we are saved just because God loved us—God loves all and yet we believe that many are lost—we know that many are unconverted.

Let us look to scripture for clarification on this matter. Jesus explains it fully in John 3:16-18. We have verse 16 memorized, but read on for what many are missing. Jesus said, "For God so loved the world that he gave his one and only Son, that whoever believes in him shall not perish but have eternal life. For God did not send his Son into the world to condemn the world, but to save the world through him. Whoever believes in him is not condemned, but whoever does not believe stands condemned already because he has not believed in the name of God's one and only Son."

Condemnation of humanity was never, and is never, God's desire. Jesus Christ did not come into the world to bring judgment on us, but rather to make freedom from judgment a reality. The essence of the gospel message is that Jesus has come to deliver humanity from the consequences of sin. That is not all God wishes to do for us—it is just the starting point.

Our assurance is found in the next verse that tells us that if we believe in Jesus Christ as our Savior we are not living the life of a condemned person. The reason is that if we trust Christ as our Savior, then we accept that He suffered the penalty of our sin. He was punished for us. We can go free because we have put all our hopes of being freed from judgment in Him—not in our own goodness.

The problem with facing a holy God, who allowed His Son to die for us, on our own merit is found in the next sentence of the verse. The one who does not believe in Christ is already condemned because he or she has rejected the only sufficient way to escape the judgment of God. No matter how good we may be, the God of the Bible only accepts His means of deliverance.

Why? Because with His method everyone has an equal chance no matter how one has lived, who one is, what one possesses or what advantage one might have. With God we all stand on equal footing in regard to our opportunity to receive eternal life. We are not accepted by God just because we are loved by God. God accepts us when we accept His gift of love—Jesus Christ.

Day 74

THIS IS NOT ALL

In my profession, I am often called upon to give words of comfort where there seem to be none to offer. At times I think that people hope that I can explain the reason for tragic events in some way as to help make sense of it all. I have met people who have an explanation for everything, but the longer I live and the more I understand the scriptures the more I realize that God does not always explain Himself, His ways, or why certain events take place.

One truth that helps me cope in difficult times is that this present reality is not all there is for me. In most cases taking a "this too shall pass" attitude is beneficial—because it will pass. It will pass because of prayer and God's intervention. It will pass simply because time makes most situations pass. Life rarely remains the same for any extended period of time.

In addition, this life is not all there is for me. I, and all who know Christ, will live for eternity. Put aside any ideas that we will spend eternity sitting on clouds and playing a harp. The scriptures reveal that we will live fulfilled and happy lives serving God, having friends and accomplishing His work all without having to contend with the difficulties that we now face.

With this, and present difficulties in mind, the Apostle Paul offers these words. "Therefore we do not lose heart. Though outwardly we are wasting away, yet inwardly we are being renewed day by day. For our light and momentary troubles are achieving for us an eternal glory that far outweighs them all." 2 Corinthians 4:16-17 NIV

Great words of encouragement, but the phrase "light and momentary troubles" might make us think that Paul failed to understand how difficult life could be for many. He obviously had never been through many trials. On the contrary, Paul had been through many trials. I have summarized a list of Paul's adventures so that we might see what he calls "light and momentary troubles."

He writes, "I have worked...harder, been in prison... been flogged...exposed to death (repeatedly). Five times I received...forty lashes minus one. Three times...beaten with rods, once...stoned, three times... shipwrecked, I spent a night and a day in the open sea... constantly on the move. I have been in danger from rivers...from bandits...from my own countrymen...from Gentiles; in danger in the city...in the country...at sea; and...from false brothers. I have labored...toiled...gone without sleep...known hunger and thirst and have often gone without food; I have been cold and naked. Besides everything else, I face daily the pressure of my concern for all the churches." 2 Corinthians 11:23-28 NIV

Either Paul was not in touch with reality or he understood a greater reality. I think it was the latter. That is why he said, "So we fix our eyes not on what is seen, but on what is unseen. For what is seen is temporary, but what is unseen is eternal." 2 Corinthians 4:18 NIV

I think he is saying that our present reality is not all there is, that there is "an eternal glory that far outweighs" anything we may be facing now. Let me encourage you to keep your eyes on what is not seen. By faith you will make it.

Day 75

WE PRAY ACCORDING TO OUR HEARTS

Have you ever noticed that it is easy to pray for some people and necessary to pray about others? I have found that there are some people that I end up praying more about than for. It seems that I am continually forced to pray about their actions instead of only praying for their well-being; and the truth is, it can be difficult to pray for people whom we do not feel have our best interest at heart. It is even more difficult to pray for people who hurt us, use us and leave us wounded without a word of regret.

Of course, the easiest road to take with these people is to just ignore them and leave them to their own devices until we are forced to deal with them in the future. After all, it is bad enough that we have to pray about them when we have a head-on encounter with them. To pray for them even when we are not forced to can be distasteful to our emotions. But the fact is that Christ did not call us to do what we felt—and not even what was always easy. Neither did He paint a permanent smile on our faces and make us immune to emotional hurts. However, for those who live for Him He did give the secret to overcoming in just such situations.

In Luke 6:27-28 Jesus gives us what some might say is unbelievable instructions. He says, "But I tell you who hear me: Love your enemies, do good to those who hate you, bless those who curse you, pray for those who mistreat you." NIV Did Jesus actually mean all that literally? He really did. In fact, it is so plain that, as someone once said, "It would take a theologian to misunderstand it."

What good could possibly come from you and me having a loving and good heart toward those who hate us and misuse us? Well, for one thing we will not be like them; we will, instead, be like Christ. But it goes further than just taking the emotional or moral high road. Too many people want to make Christianity all about rules and laws and what they can get by with, while ignoring the true essence of what it means to please God.

But Jesus put the nature of a true experience with God in perspective when He gave the two greatest commandments, "Love the Lord your God with all your heart and with all your soul and with all your mind and with all your strength.' The second is this: `Love your neighbor as yourself.' There is no commandment greater than these." Mark 12:30-31 NIV

Again, Jesus leaves us no room for debate. If we will be pleasing to God and obedient, we will have our hearts right with Him and others. With our hearts right we can now pray for those who have mistreated us and even our enemies. So, what do we pray? For starters we can pray that God will turn their hearts toward Him. We can pray for God's will to be done in their lives. And we can pray for God to keep our hearts pure so that we can truly "bless" them and seek to do good toward them without hypocrisy.

Jesus knew that not everyone would accept such a radical teaching. That is why he said in the earlier passage, "I tell you who hear me..." As always, some will hold to hurts and anger instead of to love. But let me encourage you to ask Christ to fill your heart with His love to the point that you have room for nothing else.

Day 76

OUR HEAVENLY FATHER HEARS AND UNDERSTANDS

As anyone who has or have had children in the house can tell you, crying spells are not unusual in the early years of a child's life. As infants, they cry when hungry, when they need a diaper change, when they are sleepy, when mom or dad are sleepy and just about any other time they feel uncomfortable or need anything. It gets better though—thank the Lord.

Toddlers usually cry because they have fallen or bumped their heads on any given number of items around the house. They cry when they get tired and cranky or when something is taken from them or when mom or dad refuses to give them something they want. Grandparents are the source of the latter problem—they give them anything they want.

The progression continues as the children get past the toddler stage and enter the kindergarten and elementary school years. Now, in addition to the usual upsets, they can be found crying when their feelings have been hurt. And all through these years, and many more to come, parents seem to develop a second sense concerning the many tones and sounds of their children's cry. When the parents hear the child crying, they can usually tell if it is serious or not. They know their child and can usually immediately tell the difference between being hurt and being angry, between having a fit and being scared. The only problem is that children usually want instant and satisfactory attention no matter what is happening.

Too many times when it comes to spiritual needs and our relationship with our heavenly Father we are just like these children. We demand instant and satisfactory attention and if disappointed we want to know why. But have you ever stopped to consider that our heavenly Parent knows us better than we know our own children? When we cry out to God, no matter how urgent we feel the need is, He knows instantly if we are in dire need or if we are just panicking.

The fact is that many Christians respond to God as their children respond to them. Just let children think that you are not taking their problem seriously and they will be crushed. And I see people who are crushed all the time because they did not draw the desired reaction from God. As parents, we understand things that the children do not; we know solutions and answers about which they have no clue. It is not that we do not care; we just understand the situation better. Likewise we can all rest assured that God knows all about our situation.

So, the next time you are in distress, let me encourage you to remember the words of the psalmist. "I love the LORD, for he heard my voice; he heard my cry for mercy. Because he turned his ear to me, I will call on him as long as I live. The cords of death entangled me, the anguish of the grave came upon me; I was overcome by trouble and sorrow. Then I called on the name of the LORD: "O LORD, save me!" The LORD is gracious and righteous; our God is full of compassion. The LORD protects the simplehearted; when I was in great need, he saved me. Be at rest once more, O my soul, for the LORD has been good to you. Psalms 116:1-7 NIV

Day 77

DEFEATING DEPRESSION

Depression can be deadly, but more often it simply ruins the quality of life for an individual. People who are depressed often feel sad or empty, hopeless and pessimistic, and even guilty. Feelings of helplessness or worthlessness are common. They will often find themselves unable to make decisions or to concentrate. Depressed individuals often lose interest or pleasure in ordinary activities and have increased problems at school, work or with family. A loss of energy and drive as well as restlessness and irritability are most commonly associated with depression. But some may go so far as to begin drinking heavily, taking drugs and talking about death or even suicide.

Often misunderstood, depression leaves many people of faith feeling confused and less than adequate as a believer. Worse still are those who promote the idea that those who really have faith will never be depressed. This is simply not Biblical. What is a Biblical belief is the idea that Christ will strengthen us in every state of need in which we find ourselves. (Philippians 4:13)

The fact is that James said that Elijah, one of the great heroes of the Bible, "was a man just like us" (James 5:17 NIV) and yet we know that he went through a notable time of depression. We find him in a challenging time in his life in 1 Kings 18 and 19. The great prophet has finally had enough. It did not matter that he had been successful in the past, now his mind and body was telling him that he was a failure. In his mind he might as well have been dead (19:4).

Elijah was not having a bad day. He was not even having a bad week. He was working on bad months. After he volunteers to die, God still leads him forty days into the wilderness and the depression follows him every step of the way (19:8). That is the way depression is—it hangs on—it seems that it will not let us go no matter how we try to escape it.

When Elijah finds himself spending the night in the cave it must have seemed to him that he had found suitable accommodations for himself. What better place could there be to get away from it all? Of course caves are a little hard to come by for most of us. So we just close the curtains, refuse to answer the phone, miss work and withdraw socially. And we do what Elijah did; we allow our perceptions to become our reality (19:10,14).

God was his only counselor—his only therapist—so he vented his feeling to God. In return, God listened to him, but (this might be important) refused to agree with him. To the casual reader it might even seem as if God was calloused in His response to Elijah (19:13-15). But God knew that what Elijah needed was not pity, but to know that He still had confidence in him.

God was telling him that his life was not over and his usefulness had not been lost. And that is what God wants you to know as well. If you are facing depression let me encourage you to seek out someone to help you through it. It only seems that you are alone in a wilderness. There are ministers, counselors or friends that would be happy to walk with you as you seek to leave your wilderness.

Day 78

GOD MEANS FOR US TO BE ONE

If Americans have ever considered what it is to be hated for simply existing or for being of a particular nationality, it should be now. I cannot say that my country has never done anything wrong in policy or practice, but as a whole, I do believe that what America stands for is right, noble and certainly better than what one will find in most countries of the world. Nevertheless, we are hated by many today, no matter how we attempt to do what is right. It is frustrating, is it not?

An overlooked truth is that many people have faced that feeling for centuries. Because of their national origin or the color of their skin or their race, they are thought of as evil, inferior and even worthless. No matter what they accomplish, how good they may be, their individual kindness, intelligence, and contributions are discounted because of who they are not, as well as because of who they are.

Several years ago I believe I was given a brief glimpse of what it must be like to be judged by the color of one's skin. My wife and I were crossing a reservation out west. After hours of driving across an empty desert we stopped to buy gas and get something to eat. We had not been there long before it became apparent that we did not belong. Hardly anyone would speak to us. Suspicious and unfriendly glances followed us. While the manager of the restaurant was friendly, the other patrons just watched us—perhaps out of curiosity. While seated at a table, we saw a group of people come in and take a booth near us; one woman flung a highchair into our table to get it out of her way. She then stopped and stared at us for a moment, as if she were daring us to respond.

Frankly, the general atmosphere had me concerned for our safety. We had not mistreated her nor did I have any intention of doing so. But we must have reminded those around us of others who had mistreated them. Even a casual student of history would have to admit that these were people who have been mistreated. And I knew that my skin was the same color of those who had done them wrong. In many ways they were justified in their feelings. Facts are facts.

It was a situation without easy answers. It was a situation that made me keenly aware of the unfairness of prejudice—especially the baseless kind. Years and years of feelings, ideas, prejudices and wrong actions kept us apart like a barrier that could not be breached. What a senseless waste of what Christ wants us to be.

Paul reveals God's wishes for those who will be Christians when he writes, "You are all sons of God through faith in Christ Jesus...There is neither Jew nor Greek, slave nor free, male nor female, for you are all one in Christ Jesus." Galatians 3:26-28 NIV Simply put, all the things that matter to us, that separate us and that we use to judge one another, mean nothing to God.

This is that for which Christ gave Himself. "But now in Christ Jesus you who once were far away have been brought near through the blood of Christ. For he himself is our peace, who has made the two one and has destroyed the barrier, the dividing wall of hostility..." Ephesians 2:13-14 NIV The world must make its own decisions but as for us there is no place for a "wall of hostility" in the heart of a Christian.

Day 79

WHAT I KNOW WHEN I KNOW NOTHING

The other day I was attempting to explain why I knew something about a particular situation to my daughter. Frustrated by not being able to get through to her with explanations, I fell back on a tried and true response. "Because I said it was that way." It was all I could come up with. "Oh," she said, "there are just some things that daddies know, right?" Feeling triumphant I agreed, "Yes, there are just some things that daddies know." However, after a short pause she added, "But I bet you don't know everything like mama does. Mama knows everything!"

That is pretty much the way life goes. Just when we begin to think we have it all figured out we find out that we do not know as much as we thought we did. Sometimes tragedy strikes, shaking our feeling of security. Sometimes it is financial insecurity, job related problems or relationship problems that leave us feeling as if all that we were sure about is gone. It is then that we may wonder if there is anything on which we can depend.

I have found that the one constant in my life is my Heavenly Father Himself. James reminds us that He (God) "does not change like shifting shadows." 1:17 NIV You will not find God changing with the seasons or circumstances. He remains the same. Therefore when I do not know anything about this life that is for sure, I know that God is forever the same.

I also know that God loves me, not because I deserve it, but because He wants to. Someone said that Billy Graham was asked what he thought was the greatest theological statement ever made. His reported response was, "Jesus loves me, this I know, for the Bible tells me so." The comfort of this truth is magnified by the fact that He will not change.

I know that God the Father has the ability to help me no matter what I face. Isaiah 40:28-31 asks, "Do you not know? Have you not heard? The LORD is the everlasting God, the Creator of the ends of the earth. He will not grow tired or weary, and his understanding no one can fathom. He gives strength to the weary and increases the power of the weak. Even youths grow tired and weary, and young men stumble and fall; but those who hope in the LORD will renew their strength. They will soar on wings like eagles; they will run and not grow weary, they will walk and not be faint." NIV

There are actually several things that I know when I do not know anything. And all that gives me strength and comfort and assurance, center on knowing God. My imperfections and failures limit me in countless ways, but I know that my Heavenly Father is not limited in any way. So, in all my confusion and questioning I can simply turn to Him and find peace.

Let me encourage you today to look to Him for answers and help instead of floundering in a state of confusion that will only lead you into fear and hopelessness.

Day 80

KEEPING YOUR JOY THROUGH ORDINARY DAYS

Cleaning toilets is exciting! When is the last time you heard someone say that? I have never heard it said, nor do I agree with the statement. Cleaning toilets are a necessary evil. But that is what I have been doing. Just a few hours ago I was a "featured speaker," but now it is time to clean toilets. The point is that life is kind of that way—punctuated with menial tasks and made up of ordinary circumstances. I mention this because I realize that it is not uncommon for people to want every moment of their lives to be fulfilling and challenging. The problem is, that if that is one's expectation, there are going to be disappointing days filled with ordinary duties that are less than fulfilling.

In the religious world, especially if one watches a good bit of Christian television, some may have the idea that serving God or being a Christian is all glitter and goose bumps. We see those TV Christian folks with their colgate smiles and sparkly clothes and think that they must hear from God all the time and even find great spiritual significance in making oatmeal. I would not count on it. They are human, too.

My point is that no one is able to live on a spiritual mountaintop every moment of every day. But we can be confident in knowing that our lives are not futile and even that we are being used for a greater purpose than what may appear at hand. Those who do not allow ordinary days and ordinary tasks to get them down are those who know this and rest in that truth.

These are the people with real joy. They are able to keep their joy by not depending on the excitement of life to motivate them. It is their relationship with God and the knowledge of Christ that keep them satisfied and always looking for those easily-overlooked moments when God is doing something in their life. In fact, one of the best definitions of true Christian joy is that, "Joy is the anticipation of what God is going to do."

Everyone knows that nothing will take the joy out of living like believing that we are trapped in a meaningless existence. However, based on the belief that God is always about to do something good in our lives, we can look forward to extraordinary days while living out our ordinary days. This joy is all about trusting in Christ as you and I live out our lives. Through valleys, over mountains and across the vast changeless scenery of the plains we walk on with our Lord and Savior, always knowing that a great destination awaits us, and the journey itself is molding us into what we need to be.

Paul's prayer for those who would follow Christ was, "May the God of hope fill you with all joy and peace as you trust in him, so that you may overflow with hope by the power of the Holy Spirit." Romans 15:13 NIV What a powerful prayer! Paul is pointing us to the One who is able to inspire hope, fill us with joy and peace and cause our hearts to overflow with hope through the Holy Spirit.

Nothing is left to chance. Nothing is circumstance dependant. The "God of Hope," working through the Holy Spirit, is able to inspire within us the courage to face ordinary days with extraordinary expectations. Let me encourage you today to look beyond your circumstances and find the joy that awaits you!

Day 81

BEYOND THE REALM OF HUMAN COMFORT

It was one of the most difficult things that I had ever done in my pastoral experience. The phone rang in the church office just before service time. The news was not good. The brother of one of our church members had just died from a massive heart attack at a relatively young age. The person on the other end of the phone line asked me if I would give the news to his sister. It was now my duty to break the shocking and bad news to the unsuspecting family member waiting in the sanctuary.

Upon entering the sanctuary I found the woman's husband. Taking him aside, I told him of what had happened and asked if he would bring his wife into the fellowship hall of the church so that we could break the news to her in private. Shortly thereafter she entered, and finding me and a few close friends waiting for her, she began joking that we must be up to something. I will never forget how her smile faded as we all stood somber-faced around her. No doubt she got that same sick feeling that we all had—only we knew why. The room grew quiet and then I broke the news the best I could. At that moment she walked beyond the realm of human comfort.

Although she collapsed into her husband's arms, it was evident that his embrace was of limited comfort. At that point, words meant very little. At that point, only the Holy Spirit could speak words of comfort to her—only His embrace could make a difference. Perhaps that is why the psalmist David did not include anyone else in his thoughts when he wrote, "Even though I walk through the valley of the shadow of death, I will fear no evil, for you are with me..." Psalms 23:4 NIV There are some places that only God can walk with us.

I, too, know the ability of the Lord to comfort us when we are beyond the realm of human comfort. As I sat by the graveside of my own brother, staring at the casket—the words of the minister barely registering—I heard the Lord's voice. No, it was not audible. It was really only a scripture that I had read that came to mind, but it was the Holy Spirit who reminded me of it. It was John 14:18 where Jesus said, "I will not leave you comfortless, I will come to you." I know the context. I know the theology. And I know that Jesus wanted me to know that He was there for me.

The importance and value of knowing that I was not abandoned or left to get by the best I could was what I needed, and only God's Holy Spirit could convey it to me. I was beyond the realm of human comfort, but I was not beyond His realm of comfort. At that moment I came to know an assurance that only the Lord could give.

The day will come when you or someone you love will walk beyond the realm of human comfort. It happens to us all sooner or later. But always remember the promise of Jesus Christ to those who look to Him in faith, "I will not leave you without comfort, I will come to you."

Day 82

WHERE IS THE MEANING

I have always felt that I could endure most anything, as long as I knew it mattered or there was a purpose to it all. Evidently, others feel that way too. Perhaps that is why the college student sits through interesting and uninteresting lectures alike, the cancer patient endures chemotherapy, the athlete endures rigorous training—it is part of reaching a goal.

But what about when there seems to be no goal and no meaning to our struggles—what should be our attitude then? The last thing I want to do is to try to sound like a philosopher, just the same, I would have to answer that there is always meaning and purpose to be found. In fact, it is at just such times that God often steps into our questioning and confusion and reminds us that, "We know that in all things God works for the good of those who love him, who have been called according to his purpose." Romans 8:28 NIV

Of course, I am of the theological persuasion that every act, every thought, and every word is not determined before hand by God. This in no way diminishes His sovereignty. He does not lack the power or ability or the will to change or direct the matters of our lives and even us. Paul simply wants us to know that God is at work at all times in our lives. He can take any given situation and use it for our benefit, because God sees meaning in what we see as meaningless.

It is common for us as human beings to see certain occurrences in our lives as meaningless. Consequently, it is therefore easy to see how that we may be surprised when something positive comes out of a hopeless or meaningless tragedy or situation. But remember, as a rule, meaning is only found when we seek for it. It will not always jump up and bite us. However, when we look for God's direction or listen for the voice of God, He can take those occurrences and use them to mold and shape us. Under those circumstances, it would stand to reason that God could even make the meaningless, meaningful.

The problem is that, humanly speaking; it is not always easy to see the greater meaning or greater good in every situation. Furthermore, it is not always easy to "hear the voice of God." So, the question remains, what do we do? We give every circumstance, every moment, every event to God, who alone is both able to determine what is meaningful or meaningless and who is able to work both for our good. I believe the scripture calls it submitting to the Lordship of Christ.

When we are frustrated in our minds and emotions by problems with no answers, circumstances void of hope, and we are faced with apparent meaninglessness, it is possible to have peace of mind that something good can yet take place. We arrive at this state of mind as "we take captive every thought to make it obedient to Christ." 2 Corinthians 10:5 NIV To put it another way, "Just put it in God's hands."

God is sovereign, but in His sovereignty He chose to give us the choice of whether or not we would yield everything in our lives and being to Him. Let me encourage you today to give it all to the Lord.

Day 83

TIME TO GROW UP

When my wife and I were considering the possibility of having a second child, we had several people tell us that two was just as easy to rear as one. Well, we have two now and the truth is, they were lying! Trying to care for two children instead of one, in all the ways that they need care, is more challenging in almost every way.

Do not misunderstand me. I deeply love my two little girls and I am happy to have them both. I would not trade them for good sense. They have brought love and joy into our home unlike anything we have ever known. They can melt my heart with a single look or a simple hug. They make me feel special and important. To them I am not just daddy. I am the slayer of icky bugs and things that go bump in the night. I am the one that can protect them from thunder and things that live under the bed. It almost makes me want another child. Almost.

Of course, we do not want our girls to remain children forever. As sweet as they can be, it would be abnormal for them to remain children. I am sure that even their cute words and actions would lose their charm after a few years. The natural progression of things is for them to grow and mature. Besides, there is much that they would miss if they were to remain children.

Of course, this hypothetical situation is never going to be. We all grow up physically after a while whether we like it or not. However, some have found ways to remain child-like in their emotions and, possibly worse, remain children spiritually. This is significant because many problems in relationships are caused by one or more of the people involved being immature or childish in their emotions and thought processes. Furthermore, many problems are caused in the church because of the same situation.

Often in the scriptures Paul and other writers encourage us to have the attributes of children, but when Paul had to deal with petty attitudes and narrow-minded thinking he would appeal to the problem individuals to stop being like children. For example he writes, "Brothers, stop thinking like children. In regard to evil be infants, but in your thinking be adults." 1 Corinthians 14:20

Even Peter encourages us to grow up. "Therefore, rid yourselves of all malice and all deceit, hypocrisy, envy, and slander of every kind. Like newborn babies, crave pure spiritual milk, so that by it you may grow up in your salvation." 1 Peter 2:1-2 NIV

Finally, Paul makes God's will in this matter clear when he writes, "That the body of Christ may be built up until we all reach unity in the faith and in the knowledge of the Son of God and become mature, attaining to the whole measure of the fullness of Christ. Then we will no longer be infants... Instead, speaking the truth in love, we will in all things grow up into him who is the Head, that is, Christ." Ephesians 4:12-15 NIV

Let me encourage you to examine yourselves to see if there is any childishness in your attitude or actions. If so, you may have found the source of a problem. The good news is that just working on "growing up" will bring a positive change.

Day 84

SHOW AND TELL

The other day I was searching the radio dial for some good music when I came across a country music station playing a song I had not heard in a while. Willie Nelson was singing the song, "You were always on my mind." I had never really paid much attention to that song—not being an avid country music listener—but that day I stopped and listened. Previously, I had thought that it was a nice romantic ballad. After listening to the words though, I now realize that it was obviously written by a man with little understanding of women or love.

Now, before you get the idea that I am a self-proclaimed authority on women let me set you straight. I am not—not even close. However, I know a few things the songwriter obviously does not. First of all, the words say, more or less, "I know I never told you I loved you, maybe I was not there, maybe I did not treat you like I should have, etc., but"—here is the good part—"you were always on my mind."

Well, there you go! What mistreated, lonely, affection-deprived woman would not be happy just to know that some man was thinking about her? That should make up for pretty much everything. (Pardon the sarcasm.) The fact is that sentiment like that makes for a good country song but makes for terrible relationships. People, all people, like to be told and shown that they are loved. One goes hand-in-hand with the other.

My father, who is a good man and who does love my mother, is also a man who has always struggled to express his love verbally. Once when my mother said to him, "I wish you would tell me that you loved me more." His reply was, "You got a roof over your head, don't you?" Hmmm. Long walks, intimate talks, whispers of sweet nothings and roofs! As they say on Sesame Street, "What does not belong in this picture?"

As humans we seem to go to one extreme or another. Either we talk about love and do not show it, or we show love and fail to speak of it. In 1 Corinthians 13, Paul addresses the inconsistency of human love. He also seems to have gotten right to the heart of the matter in his description of true love. "Love is patient, love is kind. It does not envy, it does not boast, it is not proud. It is not rude, it is not self-seeking, it is not easily angered, it keeps no record of wrongs. Love does not delight in evil but rejoices with the truth. It always protects,

always trusts, always hopes, always perseveres. Love never fails."
Vv. 4-8 NIV

At first glance, it might appear that Paul is purely centered on actions that show love, but if we will look closely we will see that what is said or not said in the process of showing love is equally important. True love is balanced and seeks to meet not only the material needs but also the emotional needs of the one being loved. True love is a "show and tell" proposition.

Day 85

GOD USES NOBODIES

What would you do if you had fame, fortune or power? Many are waiting until they achieve one or all of these before they attempt to make a difference in the world or accomplish a work for God. Sadly, many will never do anything significant until they stop looking for the ideal situation or ideal opportunity.

I am reminded of a story that I read or heard somewhere. It went something like this. "Once upon a time, there was a man who repeatedly said, 'If I had wealth I would give to the poor and if I had talent I would accomplish something great.' So, one day God decided to grant him his desire and give the man wealth and great talent. But as time passed the man never gave to the poor or anyone else. In addition, he did nothing with his talent. So, God decided to take the man's talent and his wealth from him. Again, the man said, 'If only I had wealth and talent, the things that I would do.' And God said, 'Oh, shut up!'"

Now, whereas I cannot imagine God saying it just that way, I can imagine God calling us on our hollow promises and weak intentions. But I can also imagine God giving us ample opportunity to impact the world and the lives of others. People often fail to see this because they fail to see themselves as being able to make a difference or as being someone God could use. They see themselves as "nobodies."

Frankly, the Apostle Paul is truthfully blunt when he addresses this very truth. He writes, "Brothers, think of what you were when you were called. Not many of you were wise by human standards; not many were influential; not many were of noble birth. But God chose the foolish things of the world to shame the wise; God chose the weak things of the world to shame the strong. He chose the lowly things of this world and the despised things—and the things that are not—to nullify the things that are, so that no one may boast before him." 1 Corinthians 1:26-29 NIV

It sounds to me like he is saying, "Folks, you were a group of 'nobodies' before you came to Christ, but God chose you because He could use you." Not being a "somebody" is rarely the problem; however, not being useable is usually the problem. The question that remains is, "Will we make ourselves available?"

"But, if you only understood," is what some would say. Others, "It is not that simple." But I say that one never knows what he or she can do when his or her trust is in God to make a way. I saved the two verses that precede Paul's words above for just that point.

Paul writes, "But to those whom God has called, both Jews and Greeks, Christ the power of God and the wisdom of God. For the foolishness of God is wiser than man's wisdom, and the weakness of God is stronger than man's strength." 1 Corinthians 1:24-25 NIV

In this passage I find these truths: no matter who we are, Jesus Christ is all-sufficient for our needs; and secondly, if we will allow Him, He can do a work through us that not even the biggest "somebody" in the world can accomplish without Him.

Day 86

WHAT IT TAKES TO BE GRATEFUL

One of the easiest things that we will ever do is to be ungrateful. Being ungrateful is easy. In fact, too often we have developed being ungrateful into a fine art. We wake up grumpy and walk around all day complaining about life, the way we feel and what we have to do. Oddly enough, it never makes us feel better to whine about how bad our lives are. But interestingly enough, focusing on the good things in life—being grateful—usually does make us feel better.

Let us see if we can get that good feeling flowing. What do we to be grateful for?

A full stomach that once was empty
A merry heart that once was broken
Full cabinets that once were barren
A laughing, playing child that was once dying
A full house that once was empty
A walking cane that is no longer needed
A warm house, a soft bed and a hot shower

Waiting in line to buy food or clothing that
could not previously be bought
Going home
Being at home
Seeing the relatives come
Seeing the relatives go
Not really needing anything for Christmas or birthdays
Hearing "Daddy!" when you come through the door
Having heard "Daddy!" in the past, even just once
Seeing old veterans meeting in buildings with
rusted tanks placed out front
Not having to pick up a pack and rifle and wonder
if you are coming back
Joys in the past
Joys in the present
Joys that will be
Volunteers at the mission
Godly mothers
Praying grandmothers
Having to be careful not to eat too much
An empty cross
An empty tomb
A clean heart
A promise that will last for eternity

What does it take to change our outlook? Often, all it takes is to be grateful for the blessings we do have. It is the ability and desire to look at one's life and see the good, however big or small that might be, and then appreciate it.

Day 87

THE MEASURE OF A HEART

A man in my church came into my office recently with an old violin case. He proceeded to open it and show me what appeared to be an ordinary but obviously old violin. The bow had formerly been strung with horsehair. The strings had certainly seen better days. Yet it still seemed to be in good condition. It had been stored away for many years in his father's closet. According to his father, he had received it as a gift years before from a man who had bought it or received it as a gift from a man who was a former slave. I love antiques and this was a find—although I did not know how much of one at the time.

After I had admired the violin for a while he said, "Look inside at the writing." Turning it so that the light from the room illuminated the inside of the violin through the soundholes, I saw what he was talking about. It was the mark of the master violinmaker. There stamped on the inside were the words, "Antonius Stradivarius"! Suddenly the old antique was an extremely valuable collectors item that many would pay a handsome price just to own. I had judged the value as far less because of my ignorance of fine musical instruments. But even as unlearned as I was about musical instruments, history had taught me respect and admiration for the name "Stradivarius."

It was then that the scripture I had heard so many times came to mind, "Man looks at the outward appearance, but the LORD looks at the heart." 1 Samuel 16:7 NIV So I found the passage and read the story. This is it in a nutshell. The prophet Samuel had been sent by the Lord to anoint the new king of Israel. Arriving at the home of David and his family, Samuel sees David's older brother. Not knowing yet whom the new king would be, Samuel's attention is drawn to David's older brother. His brother was tall and apparently an impressive manly specimen. That is why, "When he arrived, Samuel saw Eliab and thought, "Surely the LORD's anointed stands here before the LORD."

But the LORD said to Samuel, "Do not consider his appearance or his height, for I have rejected him. The LORD does not look at the things man looks at. Man looks at the outward appearance, but the LORD looks at the heart." 1 Samuel 16: 6-7 NIV

Often we determine who is able to do a work for God—and who is not able—by what we see. We also look at ourselves in the same light. Too often because of what we are not, (talented, gifted, educated, popular, etc) we disqualify ourselves from a work for God or for good. The problem is that we are limited and swayed by our superficial vision. However, the Lord does not judge by our criteria. He is only influenced by the contents of the heart.

As with ourselves, and those around us, we often underestimate our value and that of others, because, as with the old violin, we fail to take the time to look inward. For what makes us truly valuable and useful is not the outward that human eyes can see, but rather it is the inward mark of the Master that He has placed upon our hearts.

Day 88

HOW TO LIVE IN TROUBLED TIMES

Recent events in America and abroad have given us a great deal to ponder. Just when it would seem that we in America had the best of all worlds and the most hopeful prospects, our world is shaken up. Trouble has come to our homeland like we have never known in our lifetime. In addition, from what I am hearing few really know what to do with the uncertainty of our times.

But troubled times are nothing new to this old world and God's people certainly do not need to go looking for something new to help them cope. For instance, we find that the Christians to whom the writer of Hebrews was writing were facing their own set of great difficulties. According to historians, these were the people who were seeing their contemporaries thrown to the lions in the great arena. Persecution was great and death was a real possibility. But the writer of Hebrews offered them comfort, hope and encouragement in Hebrews 10:23-25 when he writes, "Let us hold unswervingly to the hope we profess, for he who promised is faithful. And let us consider how we may spur one another on toward love and good deeds. Let us not give up meeting together, as some are in the habit of doing, but let us encourage one another—and all the more as you see the Day approaching." NIV

Note the actions the writer of Hebrews encourages them, as well as us, to take in order for every Christian to remain steadfast in our commitment to Christ in the times of trouble. He tells us that we must hold firm to our faith in Christ. We have placed our trust in the Lord for times such as these. We cannot allow fear of the future and hopelessness about events to cause us to doubt. God is still in control and we still have access to His divine help. All our hopes and faith are based on the secure foundation of Christ. Even in a shaky world God remains unshaken and in control.

We must also encourage one another spiritually and emotionally. In times of crisis or uncertainty we often have a greater opportunity to show the love of God. Too often in difficult situations we tend to focus on our own needs and wants in an attempt to preserve our own individual world; but the love of God rarely shines brighter than when we show it to others in dark times. If we will take advantage of it, we will have a great opportunity to do good for God. Troubled times are one of the best times for visible Christianity.

In addition, he tells us that we must continue to gather together for worship and spiritual strength. After the events of September 11, many people returned to their churches across the nation, but within only a few months they were gone again. Even if the world crisis seems to be over we still need to draw upon the spiritual strength found in worship because there will always be personal crises that come our way. I realize that feeling pushed, pressured, and fatigued by the events of difficult days can leave us with little desire to get out one more time at the end of the week for church. However, we need the encouragement that a strong community of faith offers.

We must make up our minds that we will not become alienated from one another or isolated in our faith. We must purpose in our hearts that we will take the actions necessary to insure our spiritual stability. Remember, God is faithful. Let me encourage you to be faithful as well.

Day 89

FROM ORDINARY TO EXTRAORDINARY

In Charles Schulz's "Peanuts" comic strip, Lucy asks Linus, "Do you think people ever really change?" "Sure," replies Linus, "I feel I've changed a lot this past year." Lucy says, "I meant for the better."

I have often heard people say that they do not believe that anyone can truly change. They will concede that people often become worse, but almost refuse to believe that anyone can completely change for the better. And yet this truth, which says people can indeed change for the better, is a foundational stone of the Christian faith. It is the essence of the converted life. The one who accepts Jesus Christ as Lord and Savior not only obtains the hope of eternal life, but also of a new life here and now.

In Acts 4:13, we have an example of two men who have been completely transformed by Jesus Christ. Although this particular passage does not deal with their previous change from being sinful to being Christ-like, it nevertheless highlights what is possible through a transformed life. Note that nothing about their natural appearance was impressive; yet there was something extraordinary about them. The truth was that they had not only been followers of Jesus but that they had given control of their lives to the resurrected Lord and their lives would never be the same again.

Read what the verse says, "When they saw the courage of Peter and John and realized that they were unschooled, ordinary men, they were astonished and they took note that these men had been with Jesus." NIV I like the way the passage reads because it points out that no one could find any reason to be impressed with these two ignorant and ordinary men, and yet they were. No one could find a reason for their courage, but they had it!

This is good news for those who feel that they often come up short in life. It would seem that if the system or the world or the culture or society in general does not find its accepted qualities in you, then it wants to tell you what you can and cannot be. A superficial and shallow world will often size us up and label us "ordinary"—as if we are nothing special. But God's word tells us that we are very special even if we do not live that way. That is what spiritual redemption is all about.

Peter wrote about the redemption made possible for those who accept Jesus Christ. "For you know that it was not with perishable things such as silver or gold that you were redeemed from the empty way of life handed down to you from your forefathers, but with the precious blood of Christ, a lamb without blemish or defect." 1 Peter 1:18-19

Peter and John were transformed by knowing Jesus. It was a transformation that took place at conversion. It was meant to be obvious and powerful. Spiritually, it was so obvious and so powerful that it literally changed them for the better and not even the cynics and skeptics could explain it. Peter and John had gone from ordinary to extraordinary.

Peter beautifully illustrates the meaning of the transformation when he writes, "But you are a chosen people, a royal priesthood, a holy nation, a people belonging to God, that you may declare the praises of him who called you out of darkness into his wonderful light. Once you were not a people, but now you are the people of God; once you had not received mercy, but now you have received mercy." 1 Peter 2:9-10 NIV Now that is truly a change for the better!

Day 90

GRACE FOR LIVING—GRACE FOR DYING

As a pastor I have been asked the question of whether or not deathbed repentance was possible. In other words, can someone pray for salvation in the last moment of his or her life and find that eternal salvation and acceptance from God? I can tell you from experience that too many people want to reason the answer from the perspective of what they see to be the right answer according to the person in question. If the person has always been mean or sinful, then some say God will not hear them. If they have been a good person, then God probably will hear their prayer. That seems just, does it not? The problem with that process is that God sometimes violates our so-called "sense of justice" by his grace.

So rather than reasoning what is right or wrong based on what we may have heard or what seems to be justice in light of the life of the person in question—let us look to the scripture. First of all, God's gift of salvation is free. Secondly, it is made possible through God's grace. (Read Ephesians chapter 2) This in itself presents certain problems in our understanding of justice. As Americans our own justice system has the goal of seeing the guilty get what they deserve. I am certainly not saying that that is wrong; however, we would all agree that grace plays little or no role in its operation.

Yet, God's justice system is different; it allows for the guilty to go free. That is right. That is why Jesus Christ died on a cross. He was dying in the place of all who would accept Him as their Savior. Therefore, anyone who calls on Jesus Christ for salvation can be saved—even if they have no right to ask. (Romans 10:13)

Now that I have answered that question allow me to share this concern. My biggest concern over deathbed repentance is twofold--first that people who want to be saved will wait too late. Who knows if one will even be conscious of another chance in the last moments or days of one's life? Secondly, I am concerned that an individual that plans on waiting until the last moment is missing a better life in the here and now. Looking back over my life, I realize that it would have been impossible for me to have the life that I have now without Christ. I am not talking about possessions or positions or the like. There is much in this life I could have had and achieved, but it is what cannot be bought or sold or learned or achieved that has made the difference—the intangible. It is that which I have received spiritually though a relationship with Jesus Christ that has made everything else meaningful or worthwhile.

So, for those who have wondered and questioned if there was a chance that their loved one could have been saved in the last moments of life, I confidently tell you yes, it is possible because the grace of God makes it possible. For those who live in the fear of dying without being right with God or those who are concerned that they have the opportunity to pray just prior to death, let me ask, "What value is there in waiting to do what you feel your heart is leading you to do right now?" Let me encourage you to call upon the Lord and change your focus to living and away from dying. If you and I are ready to live for Christ, we will be ready to die.

Day 91

TAKE A DOSE OF LAUGHTER
AND CALL ME IN THE MORNING

I heard the story of a fellow pastor who had a woman in his congregation come up to him after service and ask him, "Do you watch Brother B. after church on Sunday nights?" "No, I don't, " he replied, "I watch the Three Stooges." After gasping in sanctimonious disbelief she responded, "Well you should! You should see what he does for people!" To which the pastor responded, "You should see what the Three Stooges do for me!"

While I believe that a person should be a Christian 24 hours a day, 7 days a week, I do not believe that living a Christian life means being serious all the time. I certainly do not believe that we have to be grim-faced and constantly ponder deep theological issues in order to be "spiritual." What I do believe is that we need to laugh and laugh often.

Early in my ministry I had an older minister caution me, to say the least, about using humor and joking with people. Now, I realize the danger of being offensive and inappropriate in the use of humor, and I try never to do that, but I just could not see giving up laughter because one person did not like it. A few years later, I asked another older minister about the use of humor as a minister. He responded, "You will win over more people with humor that you will ever offend." Years later I am convinced that he was right and I am glad I listened to him. Sure, I have offended some people by being happy. I have even gone so far as to actually provoke my congregation through a humorous story to laugh during church. Yes, I admit it. I am out of control.

The truth is that laughter is beneficial to the human existence. Note what Solomon writes in Proverbs. "A cheerful heart is good medicine, but a crushed spirit dries up the bones." NIV (17:22) Medical science has actually proven that there are psychological and physical benefits to laughing and having a cheerful disposition. The mind affects the body. The attitude affects the outlook.

I am not saying that if we just laugh everything will be better. Neither do I believe in just slapping someone on the back and saying, "Cheer up!" Nevertheless, I do believe that if we will focus our minds on the brighter outlook of God's Word, pray for spiritual and emotional strength, and begin to associate with cheerful and upbeat people, we might just find ourselves being able to laugh a little more often.

Be aware of the need to use humor appropriately. Try not to offend anyone. But let me encourage you to laugh all you can. There will always be too many opportunities to weep or to be serious. However, in all our busyness, if we are not careful, opportunities to laugh may pass us by. Solomon wrote that to everything there was a season, "A time to weep and a time to laugh, a time to mourn and a time to dance..." Ecc. 3:4 NIV Joy and laughter is every bit as much a part of the Christian experience as prayer. So, do not skip those opportunities to laugh—they may just be what the doctor ordered.

Day 92

INCREASING YOUR QUALITY OF LIFE

Peace of mind, prosperity, health and positive relationships are all aspects of life that we would like to enjoy. In fact, they are goals that many Americans pursue with fervor. Go to any bookstore with a self-help aisle and you will find no shortage of advice and remedies. Changing one's life in a positive way is often viewed as just as necessary, or more so, as upgrading one's computer or portfolio. One method of improving one's life recently caught my attention. It is called Feng Sui (pronounced fung shway) and is said to be the Chinese art of placement.

From what I read, people pay Feng Sui practitioners several hundred to several thousand dollars to come to their homes and arrange the furniture and furnishings in the house as well as instructing them on the color to paint each room, where to place or move windows, and more. All this is done to promote the positive flow of energy in one's home, thereby contributing to the health, wealth and general welfare of the occupants.

Once on one of those home how-to-do-it programs I heard a woman tell the homeowner that she should never build a house where the front door opened to reveal a staircase leading up to the second floor. The reason? According to this woman, this would invite spirits, evidently not good ones, to come into one's home and flow up the stairs. No. I am not kidding.

Can I tell you that if I have spirits flying around my house, the placement of the stairwell or my furniture is not my biggest problem! I'll tell you how I promote the positive flow of energy and peace in my house. I put the couch where my wife tells me to put it and I paint the walls the colors that she tells me to paint them. I have also found that it is good for my health to follow this rule.

But the Bible has yet another method for obtaining peace of mind, prosperity, health and positive relationships. Instead of starting with the house, God starts with the heart. John conveyed the principle when he wrote, "Dear friend, I pray that you may enjoy good health and that all may go well with you, even as your soul is getting along well." 3 John 1:2 NIV

If we want peace in our hearts we can look to Jesus. Jesus said, "Peace I leave with you; my peace I give you. I do not give to you as the world gives. Do not let your hearts be troubled and do not be afraid." John 14:27 NIV If we want good relationships—let the law of love rule. "Now that you have purified yourselves by obeying the truth so that you have sincere love for your brothers, love one another deeply, from the heart." 1 Peter 1:22 NIV And there is much more. But the easiest path to all we need is presented to us by Christ Himself when He pointed us to God's kingdom and will and said, "Seek first his kingdom and his righteousness, and all these things will be given to you as well." Matthew 6:33 NIV

In conclusion, if you are searching for true fulfillment and a blessed life, let me encourage you to start with your heart instead of with your house.

Day 93

WHAT IS THE TESTIMONY OF YOUR LIFE?

Perspective can be very powerful in a person's life and perspective is exactly what David had as he begins to write what would later be known as Psalm 37. In my imagination I can see David secluded in his private chambers within the palace walls. As a father advises his child about the pitfalls of life, David sits down at his writing table to share with us the lessons of a lifetime lived with God.

Perhaps, reminiscing, his mind goes back to the early years of his life when he was a young shepherd boy tending his flocks. He remembers how the Lord enabled him to fight off the bears and the lions that threatened his sheep. At night under that huge expanse of sky and stars with his sheep as his only earthly companions, he could feel the presence of the Lord as it seemed that God walked through the hills and valleys. There was nothing to fear—he was never alone.

He took that same confidence in God with him when his father sent him to inquire about the welfare of his brothers who were in Israel's army. He went to inquire about the progress of the battle between Israel and the Philistines, only to find the army of Israel cowering to the threats of Goliath the Philistine. That is a day he will never forget. He remembers his brash boldness as he declares that he will fight the giant of a man, and the dismay of King Saul, as he refuses the king's armor and weaponry. In his mind, it is as fresh as though it happened yesterday. He can still see the giant fall before him and can feel the exhilaration of victory. Nothing ever felt as powerful as when the Spirit of the Lord came upon him to do battle. And that instance was only the beginning of the great conquest for the Lord that he would witness.

His mind wanders as he sits stroking his beard, alone with his thoughts, when out of the corner of his eye; he catches a glimpse of himself in the mirror that hangs on the wall. As he turns to look at his image, he sees that his hair and beard are almost white, and he realizes that he is no longer the young shepherd boy, or for that matter the young king of yesterday. And despite his position in life, he is also aware that he has never become the man he had hoped to be, nor has he become the man that many think he is. Now a lifetime of joys and heartaches, troubles and triumphs, failures and victories show in every line on his face. He finds it strangely ironic that when he was young, all he could think about was what he was going to do for God. And now in the twilight of his life, all he can think about is what God has done for him.

Perspective is very powerful. It makes everything crystal clear. And for David, he clearly sees the goodness of God. With a deep sense of satisfaction, he turns back to his writings, picks up his pen, and begins to write these words on the paper: *"I was young and now I am old... yet I have never seen the righteous forsaken or their children begging bread."* (v. 37) NIV

If you look closely you can see that these words contain the lessons he has learned as well as, what I like to think, was the testimony of his life! *Never forsaken! Never begging!*

David was not a man who was always wishing for something else. He had sought the Lord all his life and that's why he was able to look back over his life with great confidence—not because of all that he had done or because he was a great man—but because of all that the Lord had done for him.

His testimony could have been, "I've lived a long time, I've made my mistakes and committed my share of sins; but I've never seen God forsake His people and I've never known God to let His people become beggars. All my life the Lord has been good to me, what more could I ask for in this world?"

Ultimately, all of our worldly pursuits will leave us empty and wanting; yet a relationship with the Lord will fully satisfy. Let me ask you, "If you were to look back over your life today, what would you find that truly satisfied?" David found that he knew the faithfulness of God and that was all the satisfaction that he needed. How about you? Is the testimony of your life one of dissatisfaction and inconsistency or praise and thanksgiving?

Bibliography

Day 4
Stewart Hample and Eric Marshall. 1991. *Children's letters to God.* Workman Publishing. New York, NY.

Day 6
Marriage Partnership, Vol. 12, no. 2.
Bible Illustrator Copyright © 1997-1998 by Parsons Technology, Inc.

Day 8
Corrie Ten Boom, *Marriage Partnership*, Vol. 12, no. 1.

Day 10
As quoted in Bob Phillips, *Phillips' Book of Great Thoughts & Funny Sayings*, (Wheaton, IL: Tyndale House Publishers, Inc, 1993), p. 28.

Day 11
James S. Hewett, *Illustrations Unlimited* (Wheaton: Tyndale House Publishers, Inc, 1988) pp. 291-292.

Day 14
Bible Illustrator Copyright © 1997-1998 by Parsons Technology, Inc.

Day 21
James S. Hewett, *Illustrations Unlimited* (Wheaton: Tyndale House Publishers, Inc, 1988), p. 394.

Day 22
Max Lucado, 1993. *He Still Moves Stones*, Word Publishing. Dallas, TX.

Day 24
Henry J. Kaiser Family Foundation, cited in *Harper's* (4/96). *Leadership*, "To Verify."

Day 25
John Maxwell, *The 21 Irrefutable Laws of Leadership*

Day 29
Oswald Chambers, *My Utmost for His Highest.* Barbour Books

Day 31
http://www.fox.com/temptation
Discipleship Journal, November / December, 1992.

Day 42
Oswald Chambers, *My Utmost for His Highest.* Barbour Books

Day 67
The American Heritage® Dictionary of the English Language, Third Edition copyright © 1992 by Houghton Mifflin Company.

*The ideas for devotions 15, 33 and 45 came from lectures given by Dr. Terry Johns of Lee University.